HISTORIC ROAD TRIPS

FROM DALLAS ★ FORT WORTH

Wendi Pierce

with Rick Steed

Foreword by
MIKE SHROPSHIRE

Charleston · London

THE
History
PRESS

Published by The History Press

Charleston, SC 29403

www.historypress.net

All images were taken by the authors.

First published 2010

Manufactured in the United States

ISBN 978.1.59629.081.5

Pierce, Wendi.
Historic day trips from Dallas/Fort Worth / Wendi Pierce with Rick Steed ; foreword by Mike Shropshire.
p. cm.
Includes index.
ISBN 978-1-59629-081-5
1. Texas--Description and travel. 2. Dallas Region (Tex.)--Description and travel. 3. Fort Worth Region (Tex.)--Description and travel. 4. Pierce, Wendi--Travel--Texas. 5. Steed, Rick--Travel--Texas. 6. Scenic byways--Texas. 7. Automobile travel--Texas. 8. Texas--History, Local. 9. Texas--Guidebooks. I. Steed, Rick. II. Title.
F391.2.P54 2010
976.4'5315--dc22
2010017202

For Netum Andrew Steed.

Contents

Foreword

History is more or less bunk.

—*Henry Ford*

I have always been dubious of Mr. Ford's assertion, which appeared in an interview with a Chicago newspaper in 1916. In the first place, it's a long shot that he used the word "bunk." Secondly, had he been pressed on the issue, the odds are strong that Henry Ford wouldn't have known Pocahontas from John Wilkes Booth.

In one key aspect, it's easy to sympathize with Mr. Ford (who, according to the bunk of history, would fire any employee who got caught watching a motion picture produced in Hollywood). That is, through no fault of its own, history is presented to school kids in a fashion that is almost guaranteed to repel any interest in the topic.

As a product of the Fort Worth public school system, I can remember being indoctrinated into life in circa 1870s/1880s America. According to the textbook, the only figures of consequence during those two decades (excluding Mrs. O'Leary's cow) were Rutherford B. Hayes and Samuel Gompers. I vividly recall listening to a hair-raising account of these men's initiatives while the mildew peeled off the classroom wall out of sheer boredom.

What we learned of events that shaped the contours of our own north Texas heritage was…nothing. While growing up, we were exposed to certain rumors that suggested that before the white people arrived, Fort

Worth and the territory extending westward were occupied by Indians. There is a category of our society that claims an expansive expertise in the knowledge of these times. On various occasions, I was lectured on the activities of, say, the Comanches, via what Tom Wolfe in his novel *I Am Charlotte Simmons* described as "the peculiar male compulsion to display knowledge."

Sadly, when questioned about the deeper issues of Indians, etc., the commentator would quickly switch the topic to his golf game. That's what happens when you socialize with too many lawyers. The evidence seemed overwhelming that when it came to a grasp of our regional past, it was impossible to encounter someone who had any idea what he was talking about. And then I met Rick Steed.

Steed grew up in Wichita Falls, a community best known for its tornadoes, its mental asylum and the world's shortest skyscraper. But there is more to the story of Wichita Falls, a city that was geographically placed to offer the best vantage point for some events that would shape the contours of the grandeur of Texas and the entire American West as well. Steed realized that the adventures of the men and women who experienced those times were too rich to ignore. His infatuation with the era—and the human aspect of it in particular—compelled Steed to enter a painstaking pursuit of the details of the most intriguing sagas in the annals of the development of the nation.

First he read; then he hit the highway and the farm road and, sometimes, the dirt road in his determination to produce a painstakingly accurate on-the-scene investigation of these often astonishing chapters from the past—a time when the superhuman often became the norm.

I took a one-day ride out of Fort Worth with Steed to locales like Fort Belknap and Fort Richardson. Soon, the "then" became the "now," and for those who don't believe in ghosts, take a ride with Rick Steed and you will change your mind. I told Steed, "You oughta write a book," knowing all too well that such a project is much easier said than accomplished. But he got behind the wheel, and with author Wendi Pierce in the passenger seat, in three years' time a book was born. In the genre of road trip books, this ranks with Jack Kerouac's *On the Road* and another gem, *Blue Highways*, by William Least Heat-Moon.

The details of the white settlement of Texas are often disturbing. This is a narrative frequently earmarked by torture, savagery and slaughter. It is a classic story of tribalism. Much has been about the tribalism of the Comanches, Kiowas and others. But what of the tribal heritage of the white settlers? The larger majority of third-generation north Texas Anglos vaguely identify their roots as being "Scotch-Irish." That includes me.

That being the case, most of us aren't Anglos. Rather, according to our DNA, we're Celts. That would explain the hardcore nature of the violence that occurred here. When it comes to the concept of kill first and ask questions later, nobody can top the Celts when it comes to institutional mayhem.

Julius Caesar was scared to death of them. In *Druids* by Morgan Llywelyn, Caesar describes them: "In order to appease the gods, the Celts make use of colossal figures composed of twigs which they fill with living men and set on fire. The victims were preferably criminals but if the supply failed then the innocent were used."

This is not to suggest that the cascade of white settlers who arrived in Texas in the nineteenth century was entirely of Celtic origin. Yet it is undeniable that the greater majority were a breed of natural-born killers from the hills of Kentucky and Tennessee. When viewed from the aspect of anthropological tribal proclivities, the whites and Indians who fought the Cross Timbers wars were seemingly very different peoples. Yet beneath the surface, they were very much alike. That explains the manic territorial enthusiasm for high school football, which is simply a folk ritual rich in the overt symbolism of violence and sexuality.

Thus, Rick Steed's work here tells of the ultimate battlefield confrontation, when the Celts got it on with the Mongol hordes. Related in a unique travelogue format, this is a terrific read. So sit back and enjoy the ride.

Mike Shropshire
Author of *Seasons in Hell* and six other books

Preface

Perhaps the only silver lining to a hotly contested divorce is one of the most important competitive events—to be the best parent you can be. I conscientiously exercised my child-raising skills when my kids came to spend the summer with me at Possum Kingdom Lake in the mid-1980s. They had to eat their vegetables, do their chores and, at least, rest during the hottest part of the day. I took them to the library in Mineral Wells and made them check out books for their mandatory quiet time. During one visit, I ran across a book written by an old Comanche chief. His claims of Comanche dominance seemed exaggerated, but it sparked my interest in local Indian/settler battles. Sparks flew when a buddy named Randy Harris gave me local historian Jack Loftin's map locating dozens of battles between Wichita Falls and Mineral Wells (my old stomping grounds). Always considered beautiful countryside, and perhaps for other reasons not so apparent, the Indians were reluctant to give it up. I collected and organized the data into a drive I called the Ghost of the Cross Timbers. The idea was to make more informed storytellers out of parents and grandparents so they could point to a spot along the road and entertain the kids with a little true frontier excitement.

Our lake house was also my studio; I painted local landscapes and honky-tonk interiors. I felt I'd successfully depicted a Wild West "something" that I perceived in the dancers and pool shooters, and I aimed to portray the warriors in action at the locations where they made history. Collecting these stories was more addicting than salted peanuts. I neglected my painting and hired an efficient, computer-minded Sarah Palin look-alike named Lea Ann Rector to better organize the data. Soon, my scope had grown so wide that I contemplated developing additional frontier road trips and found myself driving to a tourism convention in St. Louis.

I confronted extensive freeway construction on my way north, tempting me to return along the old military road and visit early eastern Kansas and Cross Timbers Forts. After a few missed turns, I decided that when I explored other drives I would take somebody with me, and I wanted that somebody to be a writer. More than just another pair of eyes, I needed a fresh point of view. Before 9/11, my concern was that these stories were too gruesome to be acceptable for young children. Would such violence turn off the general public? Still, my biggest problem was dullness; every way I tried to weave these accounts came out as stiff as a straw hat.

I was lucky a buddy of mine named Imo introduced me to Wendi Pierce, a talented writer with enough ivory tower time to pick up a master's in English. She also acquired plenty of "street" credibility running a trendy watering spot and grew up in Florida, where they don't teach Texas history. I took her on my Cross Timbers tour, just wind-shielding Forts Richardson and Belknap, preferring to place them in the passing landscape as accompaniment to my history.

Technically, the Red River was a Spanish/French border, but when New Orleans and San Antonio were little more than campsites, the Comanches were well on their way to carving out this and the rest of the grasslands between the Mississippi and the Rockies for themselves. They acquired their strength through horsepower because they surpassed all others in stealing, breeding and fighting on the backs of these animals. A dozen or so years earlier, they joined their Ute cousins in Taos in the hopes of getting some of the wonderful Spanish "giant dogs" that were beginning to show up on the plains. For the next century and a half, they prospered, raiding and trading at the expense of surrounding European and native nations alike. One by one, all submitted or withdrew, leaving only the United States and its new line of forts along present-day I-35.

Twenty thousand Americans moved into Texas before Independence. John Graves describes in *Goodbye to a River* how, in early confrontations with Anglos, the pushy Comanches found a people that pushed back. A string of unexpected Texas Ranger victories made it possible for Fort Worth to anchor the U.S. line along the entrance of the Cross Timbers.

Twenty-five years of fighting, at the cost of seventeen lives for each mile advanced, earned this beautiful countryside the designation of "America's Deadliest Frontier." Then again, I am prejudiced. I am from here. My great-great-grandfather, Isom, brought his wife, Jane, and their son, Netum, here at the end of the Civil War to join his cousins. They hauled buffalo hides, ranched and ran a store and a mill. I felt obligated to spotlight this history, though I am mindful of how unattractive, by today's sensitivities, we come off in what Graves calls "what we did to them and they did to us." I feared that beneath our puffed chests beat hearts that knew it wasn't just our bravery that defeated the Indian but rather our diseases, technology and exploding population (600,000 at secession). This embarrassment might result in our ignoring, even forgetting, important events. Worse, like Tarrant County's Bird's Fort and Village Creek, urban sprawl would eliminate whatever enchantment these locations possessed.

I explained to Wendi that my drive is the northern part of the Texas Forts Trail and that I intended to explore the rest of the trail, as well as the others composing the early Texas settlements. She composed a narrative for each trail, portraying us and our legacy with a kind, generous hand seldom employed by one armed with magnum-caliber intelligence and wit. We ended up with nine back road drives in the shadow of the interstates for those who aren't in too much of a hurry to have an appreciation of history and an appetite for home-cooked plate lunches with a choice of two vegetables.

Rick Steed

Rick and Wendi would like to thank Alex Hughes and LeaAnn Rector: without your patience and your tireless efforts, including late nights and tight deadlines, we know that this book would not have come to fruition. Wendi would also like to thank her husband, Reese, for encouraging her to pursue this project from the first day of their very first road trip (a thousand times!).

Parker's Fort

W e started out this day trip heading southeastward on Highway 287 to Mansfield. This town developed when, in Fort Worth in 1857, two entrepreneurs, Ralph Man and Julian Feild, sold their primitive water-powered gristmill and sawmill and moved their operations about seventeen miles south. There they developed the first steam-powered gristmill in an area truly cloaked with a fabric of amber waves of grain. The town of Mansfeild, as it was originally spelled, developed around the mills of these two men, one of whom operated a general store and served as postmaster for their budding new town.

Unable to resist the town of Venus, we ventured south on Farm Road 157. This town was named for a local physician's daughter, and in the 1890s it was, for a short time, the most prosperous town in Johnson County. According to legend, when all but the drugstore had closed, the residents each pitched in five dollars to keep the last floundering business in Venus from closing its doors. FM 157 conveys its passengers around curves and right angles and through truly vast oceans of green farmland; our car was like a wayward sailboat pressed here and there by the water when the wind is still. This deep green sea meets the sky along the horizon, endless miles away. This road is an unavowed treasure, just a few minutes from the sprawl that we call home, where there are four gas stations at every junction, the colors of neon beer signs distract our eyes and the insidious smell of salty fried food rises out into the air to swindle us.

We were tossed ashore onto Highway 66 in Maypearl, and terra firma was solidified by the presence of a sign in the window of the Busy Bee ("BYOB"), hailing residents to bring themselves to Tammy and John's party at the back of the Bee. There is some disagreement about how this town got its name. It began as Eyrie (a large bird's nest) in 1903. Then the name was suddenly changed to Maypearl for either the two daughters of a railroad executive, May and Pearl, or for the wife of an official, whose maiden name was Maypearl. Whatever the case may be, there is something genteel in the sound of its name, like the memory of times long gone, and we were drawn to take a look. We turned southward onto Farm Road 308, past the Bee Creek Ranch, and while I absorbed the electric yellow of several thousand sunflowers along the road, a literal swarm of grasshoppers crashed unaware into our windshield. I was startled back to the here and now by the loudly abrupt splatter of at least twenty of these poor fat-bodied victims, whose remains obstructed our view until we could stop to clean the glass. The open road is full of odd little surprises—quick reminders to wake up or check our pulse or, more importantly, the gas gauge.

In Milford, we stopped to take a picture of the Baroness Inn Bed and Breakfast, and while we were doing so, the owner came outside to say hello. The aqua-colored building captured our attention. It's a two-story Victorian structure with a bright pink-trimmed balcony and porch. One side is shaded by an enormous tree, whose branches reach out as if for an embrace. We drove around the block to get a look at the back of the inn, which is also shaded and private. In 2003, the *Dallas Observer* voted this spot the best place for a day trip in Texas. It stands out from any other bed-and-breakfast seen; it's colorful, and the proprietors are anxious to fling open their doors for potential guests.

We turned onto Highway 171 in Malone and drove through expansive fields with very little evidence of human occupation. A barn house every few miles and the fences that line the roads serve as subtle reminders of the time when the early settlers arrived—a time when, in emergencies or Indian attacks, it took all night to reach the nearest neighbors. We passed through Hubbard, a small town that grew around the Cotton Belt train depot that was originally located there. Today it's a placid little town, one in a series of islands that dot this region's oceans of green. On calm seas we sailed into Limestone County, the great stage on which some of the most tumultuous scenes of Texas history are replayed.

John Parker, an elder in the Predestinarian Baptist Church, left Illinois to settle in Texas in 1834 intending to spread the word of the Baptist Church to those who had not yet heard. He brought his wife, "Granny" Parker, two sons, Silas and Benjamin, and four grandchildren. Samuel Frost and his son also accompanied the Parkers on their quest in March of that year. For protection from the natives that controlled this area, they built a fort in Limestone County along the headwaters of the Navasota River. It had log walls that were twelve feet high and two blockhouses on opposite corners to offer a view of far-off distances and warn the occupants of approaching danger. For lodging, there were six small cabins inside the fort's walls.

When John and his wife, Sarah, first built Fort Parker, it housed a company of rangers from time to time as they were dispatched in the area to confront the Indians—either to retrieve stolen livestock or avenge the death of a fellow frontiersman. One company, under the command of Captain Robert Coleman, sought a fortress there in July 1835 when the

A blockhouse at Parker's Fort.

Tawakoni village it attacked proved to be surprisingly resilient. Colonel John Moore answered Coleman's cry for help with three companies of rangers under his command. In August, the combined forces left Fort Parker and headed northwest, following a similar path to the one that we used for our approach to the fort. They found the village abandoned, and one ranger, Major Erath—who would soon establish the city of Waco—noted that the Indians were forced to leave behind a great store of crops, including sixty acres of corn.

Even though the Parkers and their extended family were far more prepared than most of the early settlers in Texas, their name and the misfortunes that befell them eventually became a significant part of the legend of the old frontier. I've noticed that anyone who knows the slightest bit of this area's history can't rattle off the names of Cynthia Ann and Quanah Parker without their eyes first glazing over as they wander backward into the days of Mrs. So-and-So's seventh-grade history class. Here's why.

On May 19, 1836, long after Coleman and Moore's ranger battalion had disbanded, more than one hundred Indians from Comanche, Kiowa and Wichita tribes appeared at the gates of the fort to ask for beef and directions to a water source. They were waving a white flag. Most of the men who could defend the fort were not inside those twelve-foot walls; they were working in the surrounding fields. Old John Parker and his sons were inside, so Benjamin slowly opened the heavy gates to hear their requests. He went back inside the fort to relay this conversation to the others. When he returned to the gates to talk to the warriors, planning to send them toward water and deny them a cow, they quickly drove their lances through him and charged the open gates before they could be closed.

What followed was a bloody, violent storm like nothing these Baptist immigrants had ever seen. The Indians reportedly pinned their victims to the ground with their lances, mutilated and murdered the men and raped the women, including Granny Parker. They took five captives: young Cynthia Ann and John Parker, James Plummer and two young ladies, Elizabeth Kellogg and Rachel Plummer. Though none would welcome such a title, these were the first white captives taken by Indians in Texas. Elizabeth Kellogg was taken by the Caddoans when the raiding band split their ranks, and she was soon traded to agents in Nacogdoches for

$150. Rachel Plummer and the children traveled with the Indians all the way to eastern Colorado, where she, too, was eventually ransomed. Little John Parker and James Plummer remained for six years in captivity before they were ransomed in 1842. Cynthia Ann alone assimilated to her new way of life and rose to become a Comanche leader named Naduah. Her story becomes legend because she was adopted into a Comanche family, and as she matured, she assumed the role of wife to the mighty chief Peta Nocona. The Comanche men practiced polygamy, and it is a great testament to their relationship that Nocona never took another wife.

Cynthia Ann embraced the Native American culture, and she prevented several of the whites' attempts to rescue her. She and Chief Nocona had three children; her firstborn son, Quanah, arose to become the most revered of Comanche chiefs. It is curious that one small captive child from a prominent local family could so win the hearts and respect of the Comanches that she would become the only wife of one great chief and the mother of his successor. When she was returned to the Parker family after twenty-four years with the tribe, she resisted vehemently, trying a few times to escape. Cynthia Ann's tale twists the classic "Cowboys and Indians" story so that there can never be the clearly defined lines of hero and villain, no white horse and black horse. In this great legend that describes the beginning of the Texas frontier, the heroes are those whose indelible courage and tenacity have etched their names into the books of history and not merely those who ended up with the land.

When we visited the site of Cynthia Ann's abduction, it was a sunny, breezy July day, and there were a few families of children, parents and grandparents spilling eagerly out of minivans to pay their fees and enter history. We walked through the museum and souvenir store to the fort's grounds on the other side. A wooden walkway lined with the vines of wild grapes conveyed us toward those famous gates, where in just a few moments' time the fate of the Parker clan was inexorably altered. In a fitting juxtaposition of past and present, a long-haired man on a riding lawn mower nodded his head upward and gave us a perfunctory smile as we walked toward the fort's entrance.

I know it is a reproduction of the original, but the fort is designed to enable a realistic journey into the past. A large commemorative marker within a garden of unruly flowering vines and shrubs tells the story of that day in May 1836. I was able to block out the roar of the lawn mower on the other side of the logs and the exuberant utterings of the children behind me and envision that day when Benjamin Parker, his elderly father at his side, trusted the universal meaning of a white flag and opened those gates. I could picture him glancing at his children who, with wide curious eyes, clung to the skirts of their Granny while they strained to see what waited beyond those thick logs. I could see him nervously straightening up his courage, drawing in a slow, deep breath, drying his palms on the sides of his pants and, receiving a cautious and silent nod from his father, pulling back those heavy doors.

Like Pandora's box, those doors opened under the guise of the seemingly innocuous, but they unleashed the catalyst for a series of events that would forever color the relationship between the whites and the Indians in Texas. For this was a motley mix of renegades from several tribes, not one claiming prominence over any other. In December of that year, in spite of all his efforts, President of the Republic of Texas Sam Houston could not get Congress to pass any bills granting rights for the friendly, peaceful Cherokee tribes in the East. The bitter sentiment washed over Texas, and the damage was irreparable for all sides. We walked back through the gates, and as we crossed the wooden walkway, I noticed a fiery red wasp suspended in the air beside a cluster of purple grapes. He lingered there, a flashing warning.

The clerk inside the gift shop gave us the rundown of scheduled events, from storytellers to reenactments, but she had to politely excuse herself before too long—"You know how it is when you're making jelly." On our way back up, we drove through Groesbeck's town square, snapping a picture of the courthouse while two inmates in striped jumpsuits mowed the lawn.

Highway 164 westward carried us toward Waco through Mart, whose founders—like the sparkle in the eye of the parents who see visions of a future president or military hero when they look at their infant child— named their fresh new town with the expectations of a booming commercial hub. The modern Mart, Texas, has fewer than two thousand residents, and their original dreams of grandeur faded when the railroad packed up and moved a little farther on down the road. And a little farther we went as well, to our next planned stop, the Texas Ranger Museum in Waco.

We crossed the Brazos, turned northward on University Parks Drive and entered the grounds for the museum. On rich carpets of grass sits

Major George B. Erath's statue, and we snapped a picture of it before we went inside. Erath participated first in the company of Colonel Moore when he joined forces with Coleman's rangers at Parker's Fort; then Erath served in the Battle of San Jacinto, when Texas won its war for independence, and after that he continued to serve Texas as a legislator and ranger. He was born in Vienna, Austria, but his colleagues donned him "The Flying Dutchman" after an Indian battle in Moore's ranger company, during which his young horse became so incensed by the battle cries that he rushed ahead of the others. When he was seventy-three years of age, blind and in poor health, Erath dictated the details of these events to his daughter, who recorded and compiled his memoirs. He was an honorably outspoken man, for he believed that the Mexican army, under the command of the stubborn and unpredictable Santa Anna, deserved much more credit for its courage than it received. In one section of his memoirs, he recalls that while the rest of his battalion guzzled the crates of champagne, stacked into a pyramid and left behind by the Mexican army after its defeat at San Jacinto, "I took my carouse in eating sugar." Erath's colorful accent was one of his best-known traits, and fellow ranger Noah Smithwick quoted him as saying, in a description of his own skills as a military commander, "I knows but vone vord of command, und dot ish, 'Sharge poys, Sharge!'"

We paid the five-dollar fee and entered the corridors of the hall of fame. In standard slow and silent museum-gazing cadence, I moved through the rooms, surveying glass cases displaying weapons like the Winchester repeating rifle and the Colt revolver. This particular pistol finally began to level the playing field for the rangers in their battles against the Comanches, who were fierce and deft horseback warriors. Prior to the development of the Colt revolver, the rangers had to dismount and fire their weapons from a stationary position, often using their horses as shields, while the Comanches were mobile, exact archers. Two young boys, about the size of second graders, stood with gleaming eyes in front of these cases full of guns. Their eager fingers pointed from weapon to weapon, leaving sticky smudges on the glass. One made the wet-mouthed arcade game sounds of guns firing, while the other stood anxiously beside him.

I eased past their spray of invisible bullets and their brilliant admiration of this place and surveyed the cases of uniforms and

The Erath statue at the museum.

documents, eventually coming to a display of badges. Legend claims that the early rangers cut their star-shaped badges out of Mexican coins while they rested by the fire at camp. While this version is more than unlikely, they did indeed forge their badges out of Mexican silver dollars, though gunsmiths and blacksmiths did the work. It's funny how these heroes of the old frontier, these restorers of peace and righters of wrongs, have taken on immortal powers as time goes by. When the rangers first organized into battalions to protect the whites from Indian raids, the settlers took on the burden of feeding them and occasionally providing water or shelter from the elements, and they complained about having to share a few chickens and a bushel of corn with these rough, rowdy, irregular wanderers. Somehow, as history played itself out, they became powerful enough to cut stars out of silver coins with their bare hands.

They did, however, earn their place in the ranks of historical heroes. There was the one company of volunteers—the only group of men who would respond to the pleas for help coming from Colonel Travis and his men who were tucked inside the Alamo while they heard the thunderous marching from a Mexican force of 5,000. Surely they knew their fate, but the Gonzales Ranging company answered this call, making the total number of defenders a mere 190. The rangers also took on the "disagreeable duty" of arresting fence cutters when the farming population increased and the free ranging cattlemen found their herds cut off from water by the sharp sting of barbed wire. A marker outside the entrance to the museum describes the rangers' call to once again civilize the frontier when this feud erupted.

The hall of fame contains a diverse collection of memorabilia, representing the historical, the modern and even the televised "pop culture" renditions of the Texas Rangers. I scanned the place once more before we reemerged into the bright sunlight, noting the saddles on wooden stands, several western paintings along the wall and even the massive, bulky torso of a buffalo.

Noticing on the map how close we were to Crawford, Texas, we decided to take a short detour to see the town that houses President Bush's 1,600-acre ranch, also named the Western White House. We headed down Highway 185 via Ocee. Just east of town, there is a ford in the Middle Bosque River where Crawford's original settlement began in

Swimmers at Wasp Creek.

the 1850s. A man named Nelson Crawford graded this crossing. In 1867, this burgeoning town's inn became an early station along the Brownwood stage route. Just four years later, a post office was established, and by 1890, the town had several stores, a cotton gin, steam mills for both flour and corn and four churches. The oldest building standing in Crawford's downtown area today was built in 1894, with S.E. Powell & Son's General Store on the first floor and a Masonic Lodge on the second. Now, the building houses a gift store, and Crawford's official website proudly recalls a recent visit from John Howard, the prime minister of Australia, in 2003. There he purchased a gift for Tony Blair's fiftieth birthday: a coffee mug bearing the slogan "Friends and Allies" while four adjacent flags (Spain, Australia, United States and Britain) appear beneath.

We drove slowly through town, each business waving a flag and often a picture of George W. Bush. The power plant just outside the downtown area happily hails passersby with a sign that reads, "Proudly supplying electricity to our President and First Lady." We passed a fuel station that doubles as a small café and burger shop, where the president stopped for coffee once on his way to the golf course. Their sign is blue and white, declaring "The Home of President George W. Bush." The town of Crawford is thrilled to be the president's Western White House, and every place I looked they exuded a hospitable pride in their newfound economic growth and, occasionally, their nationwide media attention. What started as a little river crossing 150 years ago is now a stopping place for foreign diplomats and the network news, just nine miles off the beaten path.

On our way back toward Highway 6, we passed two cool, inviting spots where swimmers and sunbathers took advantage of the rock-lined Wasp Creek. The water rushed across jagged rocks, forming a white foamy spray that looked hard to resist on a day like this. We stole a few pictures of these folks at their leisure while kids scrambled past one another to achieve the highest point on the rocks from which to dive. When we reached Valley Mills northwestward on Highway 6, the "Gateway to Bush Country," I noticed a panoramic view of the landscape that captured my mind. From behind thin rows of cedars I could see distant hills rising. Their shaggy tree-covered surfaces were a sharp contrast to the smoothly plowed fields in the foreground, where equidistant rolls of hay sat dormant and still after the sweaty labor of humans was complete. The only motion in this scene was the steady tilt from side to side of giant buzzards in flight—two or three flaps of those sturdy wings and then tilting and gliding, cruising a deep blue sky after days of rain.

We emerged on Highway 6 into Bosque County and through Clifton, the "Norwegian Capital of Texas." It was first named Cliff Town in reference to the limestone cliffs that surround the area, and a prosperous flour mill and limestone mill became the first commercial endeavors. The people of Clifton are proud of their Norwegian heritage, and they host a Christmas festival every year to display their cultural food and crafts. We drove through the center of town, noticing a busy spot, the Bunkhouse BBQ. We passed a historical marker for the Election Oak, where in 1854 seventeen of the twenty-one votes cast in Bosque County's first election were polled under this tree. This venerable oak still stands next to the Clifton Livestock Company.

A short leg on Highway 22 will lead you onto Highway 144 toward Meridian. This town was the childhood home of famous Texas folklorist

John A. Lomax. Because of its proximity to the Chisholm Trail, Meridian offered young Lomax access to old cowboy ballads—the vast, echoed yodeling to their herds—and black chants and labor songs. When he was a child, he developed an affinity for this regional music, and by the age of twenty, when he left home, he had compiled written records of the songs he grew up listening to. A log kitchen is all that still stands of Lomax's boyhood home, and a roadside marker in a picnic area nearby commemorates this place.

After he left his hometown, Lomax traveled around Texas collecting folksongs from a variety of sources. In order to get the authentic lyrics, he performed his research in bars and on back roads. The Handbook of Texas Online gives a good account of Lomax's endeavors, and the product of his travels was first published in 1910:

> In the back room of the White Elephant Saloon in Fort Worth he found cowhands who knew many stanzas of "The Old Chisholm Trail." A Gypsy woman living in a truck near Fort Worth sang "Git Along, Little Dogies." At Abilene an old buffalo hunter gave him the words and tune of the "Buffalo Skinners." In San Antonio in 1908 a black saloonkeeper who had been a trail cook sang "Home on the Range." Lomax's first collection, Cowboy Songs and Other Frontier Ballads, was published in 1910. Often accompanied by his son, Alan, he visited prisons to record on phonograph disks the work songs and spirituals of black inmates. At the Angola prison farm in Louisiana, he encountered a talented black minstrel, Huddie Ledbetter, better known as Leadbelly. Upon Leadbelly's release from prison, Lomax took him on a tour in the north and recorded many of his songs.

John Lomax's passion for this music is rooted deeply in his childhood, and his collection and preservation of American folk songs became his life's work. Driving through Meridian, Texas, I can only wonder what this starry-eyed young boy with a soulful heart and cleverly acute ears looked like as he stooped behind a barn or a tree stump or strained his neck out his bedroom window at night to catch every nuance of the music of the old frontier.

Modern Meridian's calendar has a busy schedule of events, from the Bosque Valley Arts and Crafts Festival to the "Top of the Hill Country" National Championship Barbecue Cook-Off, and in October, they're dancing in the streets!

We continued on 144 through Glen Rose, where drivers pass through scenic Dinosaur Valley. Just as we crossed the county line, I noticed two giant twin hills that disappear and reappear as the road rises up out of the thicket of trees along its borders. There is a roadside marker for the dinosaur tracks found in the limestone in the bottom of the Paluxy River. There are tracks from three types of dinosaurs, and they are so large that they serve as catfish traps when the river's water runs low.

Our final stop on this quick day trip was the site of Squaw Creek, where several Indian fights took place. There was a live oak with a forked trunk there that allowed for a young boy to be positioned as a lookout. On one occasion, when Indians raided a nearby household and stole a week's worth of laundry, Captain William Powell placed his son in the tree to watch. A group of citizens watched all night when, just before sunrise, as they were about to give up their post, the Indians came through. A bloody fight followed as the men of Hood County began to shoot the Indians' horses so they could engage them on foot. The Indians held their position in a ravine all day when, finally, a heavy rainstorm forced them out to face the group of whites that had grown to nearly seventy-five men. All seven warriors were killed.

In a Civil War–era battle, twenty-five Indians were vanquished by the cavalry near Squaw Creek after they killed Rigman Bryant while fox hunting. Because so many of the frontier's men and boys were occupied in the war, the women in this area disguised themselves as men so they would not appear so vulnerable to raiding warriors.

This trip through the Squaw Creek region carried us eventually to Granbury, where Highway 51 brought us home. This short drive to Fort Parker and back is a simple, U-shaped escape from the everyday grind. On the day we took this drive, it was a nearby opportunity for us to let our imaginations enter history while our senses took in the treasure-filled countryside. Permanently altered by her capture, Cynthia Ann Parker went on quite a road trip herself, and I'm sure each river and creek, limestone cliff and forked live oak had meaning in her memories. We can drive past those spots today, if only to imagine.

Forest Trail East

The map for the Texas Forest Trail region intrigued us. Set on a background of pine green, its red route curls and drifts, forming a fun-looking maze through the east Texas pines. Since our trips begin in Fort Worth, the Forest Trail's halfway point is also its southernmost point, just twenty to thirty miles due north of Houston. Upon closer inspection, we also soon realized that the route was designed with little regard for traveling time, as it makes pendulous swings out east and west, scoffing in the face of the rule about the shortest distance between two points.

However, if we have learned one thing from our on-the-road experiences, it's that we are not concerned with such petty hindrances as time. The way the map is printed, as many as twenty cool blue reservoirs sparkle alongside the swirling red trail, so scanning this page with your eyes is like a continuous refrain of "Over the River and Through the Woods." So I guess you could say that the course of our road trip was determined by the appearance of a map.

It takes a good hour and a half to two hours to drive far enough east out of the Dallas/Fort Worth metroplex to begin the trail. We picked it up at Highway 11 in Sulphur Springs. First stop, where Highways 11 and 271 intersect, is Pittsburg, Texas, named after its settlers from Georgia, the W.H. Pitts family. Right at the turn of the century, Reverend Burrell Cannon and a few investors from Pittsburg formed the Ezekiel Airship Company. This Baptist minister was determined to build a replica of the aircraft that Ezekiel describes in the Old Testament. A roadside marker in town describes Cannon's ship as having "large fabric-covered wings powered by an engine that turned four sets of paddles," which would surely look to us in this age of rocket science like a contraption from a Dr. Seuss book. This experimental craft is said to have risen only a few feet off the ground in 1902, just one year before the Wright brothers perfected the innovations of flight. The Pittsburg Optimist Club reproduced a model of the Ezekiel Airship in the 1980s, and it is on display in the Depot Museum.

The Forest Trail turns south in Daingerfield, and as you enter into town, a sign declares it to be the "4th oldest town in Texas." The Caddo Trace crossed through this area; it was an Indian path for hunting and trading that connected two rivers, the Arkansas and the Red. This Caddo route probably came very near, if not intersected, the Cherokee Trace, which ran through Pittsburg. A resourceful Cherokee hunter dragged animal hides behind his horse to flatten the grass and forge this primitive road. The work of these original trailblazers became useful to the white settlers, both for their migration into Texas from the eastern states and for their mail and stage routes once they arrived and established towns. It is ironic that the Indians literally "paved" the way of the white pioneers who would inevitably covet their possession of priceless Texas land.

These pioneers who came into Texas from the East would have crossed the path of the Forest Trail in several places, beginning at Nacogdoches and moving northward from there. They used river routes from Shreveport, or piney trails from Natchitoches, Louisiana, and New Orleans. *Journey through Texas*, by Frederick Law Olmsted, is a firsthand journal of one doctor's voyage from the northeast to the Rio Grande. He witnessed several of these "immigrant trains" making their way into Texas, and he described his observations with candor and detail:

> *Inexorable destiny it seems that drags or drives on, always Westward, these toil-worn people. Several families were frequently moving together, coming from the same district, or chance met and joined, for company, on the long road from Alabama, Georgia, or the Carolinas. Before you come upon them you hear, ringing through the woods, the fierce cries and blows with which they urge on their jaded cattle. Then the stragglers appear, lean dogs or fainting negroes, ragged and spiritless. An old granny, hauling on, by the hand, a weak boy, too old to ride and too young to keep up. An old man,*

heavily loaded, with a rifle. Then the white covers of the wagons, jerking up and down as they mount over a root or plunge into a rut, disappearing, one after another, where the road descends. Then the active and cheery prime negroes, not yet exhausted, with a joke and a suggestion about tobacco... One of these trains was made up of three large wagons, and a gang of twenty able field hands. They travel ten or fifteen miles a day, stopping wherever night overtakes them. The masters are plainly dressed, often in home-spun, keeping their eyes about them, noticing the soil, sometimes making a remark on the crops by the roadside; but generally, dogged, surly, and silent. The women are silent, too, frequently walking to relieve the teams, and weary, haggard, mud be-draggled, forlorn, and disconsolate, yet hopeful and careful. The negroes, mud-incrusted, wrapped in old blankets or gunny-bags, suffering from cold, plod on, aimless, hopeless, thoughtless, more indifferent than the oxen to all about them.

By way of long, tiring miles and harsh conditions, these easterners became the first to build towns in Texas. It seems that their courage and perseverance were the catalysts that set into motion a chain of events that we can now regard as Texas's unique history.

From the town of Lone Star, we took Highway 729, spanning the length of the giant Lake O' the Pines and eventually bringing us to Jefferson. This road is darkened on both sides by the tall, stately trees that form both a curtain to conceal the great lake from spying drivers and nearly a canopy overhead. We curved sharply through this shaded highway, passing along the way a marker for the Nash Iron Works.

The marker's text struck me as humorous. It begins to describe what seems to have been a successful endeavor for Jefferson S. Nash, who came to east Texas in 1846:

He found much iron ore, wood for charcoal, and clay to make molds. From ridge back of the furnace, charcoal and ore were poured down the smokestack. Under the furnace grate, melted iron collected in a puddle, to be put into molds for shaping farm tools, cooking pots, smoothing irons, and—in the Civil War—cannon balls and possibly guns.

But it appears that the odds were stacked quite unfavorably against him, as is summed up in the final sentence: "Nash had difficulty securing machinery, workers, capital, and transportation." Perhaps the only tangible things Jefferson Nash had was an abundant supply of iron ore and wood, and these he molded and mixed with a truckload of ambition and a dream.

We continued to Highway 49, where right at the intersection sits the roadside marker for an 1854 blacksmith shop that became a bell foundry. Here, four miles west of Jefferson, they manufactured cowbells and, later, plows.

We drove into Jefferson, Texas, at about 3:00 p.m. It was way past lunchtime, and we were hungry for catfish. Rick parked our car, "Fort DeVille," next to three classic beauties just lounging in the sun. Like sufficiently accessorized teenagers who take monochromatic matching all the way to the level of socks and earrings, with not a hair out of place, these cars sported upholstery and giant fuzzy dice to match the vibrant turquoise or yellow or red of their exterior paint. Freshly waxed, without a speck of dust, and gleaming in the bright Texas sunlight, these giddy girls of the in-crowd proudly, but implicitly, mocked the others on the block. A few squashed bugs and mud splatters never looked so bad.

We walked into the first restaurant in sight, The Bakery, which sits adjacent to the Excelsior House Hotel. The place was empty, but it had all the evidence of a busy lunch just an hour or two before. Tables and chairs were in disarray, and a wet rag lay on a table in the corner, where cups of melting ice and silverware waited to be picked up. We were greeted by a friendly woman with girlish curls in her chin-length brown hair. I scanned the menu for catfish while one eye wandered over to the glass case full of baked desserts on the other side of the cash register. Our hostess was excited to report that catfish was "on special" today, so we sat down to eat.

I looked around the restaurant; one wall was made of exposed brick and the other of wood paneling, and there were at least fifty framed photographs covering both. While I sized up the autographed photo of George W. Bush on a ski boat, I noticed that an overweight, caramel-colored, one-quarter pit bull (the other three, mutt) entered through a side door that was propped open to let in the breeze and slipped straight into the kitchen, unnoticed by all except the young girl who was back there, scarf over her hair, preparing two catfish specials. I could see part of the kitchen from where I was sitting, and I watched as the dog postured himself at the young cook's feet, waiting for a bite he clearly did not need, but to no avail. I decided to keep an open mind, even though

I squirmed a little at the idea of a dog in the kitchen. The girl at the counter asked where we were from and, upon hearing that our interest was in historic road trips, enthusiastically seized the opportunity to tell a couple of strangers about the secrets of Jefferson, Texas.

"Well, we're in a small county, so we don't have the oldest operating courthouse in Texas. That's in Linden, where I'm from." She paused to think for a few seconds. "But we're definitely the most haunted town in Texas." Okay I'll bite—now she's got my attention.

"The Jefferson Hotel is haunted. There's a ghost that lives there. Jodie Breckenridge has these ghost walks on Friday night. There's gonna be one tonight," she said with an absent-minded pause. "You should go."

"Have *you* seen the ghost?" I ask her.

"No, but my mom and stepdaughter went a couple of weeks ago. You get to carry lanterns around; they said it was real fun. Ghosts'll show up on those digital cameras."

"Do you have any idea who the ghost might be?"

"No." Her face lights up as a new idea occurs to her. "But Diamond Bessie was murdered here [in Jefferson]."

In the 1870s, the east Texas courts saw the kind of sensationalism that became the precursor to our media circuses today. Diamond Bessie's murder trial was one of the most famous trials in Texas and likened to the O.J. Simpson drama by some. It all began when a traveling jewelry salesman and his wife registered their names at the Brooks House hotel in Jefferson, Texas. They signed in as "A. Monroe and wife," but two days prior they had stayed in Marshall under the name "A. Rothschild and wife." It turns out that they were never married, and their real names were Abraham Rothschild and "Diamond Bessie" Moore, a well-known prostitute who worked in brothels in Cincinnati, New Orleans and, finally, Hot Springs, Arkansas, where she met Rothschild. She was pretty and well dressed, and legend has it that she got her nickname because so many of her male clients bestowed on her gifts of expensive jewelry.

The curious townspeople last saw the elusive pair on a Sunday morning crossing the bridge over Big Cypress Creek, picnic lunch in hand. Mr. "Monroe" returned alone from that picnic, and he left town two days later carrying both sets of luggage. A little more than a week after Bessie's disappearance, Jefferson citizen Sarah King found her body, with a gunshot wound in her head, and the remains of their picnic lunch.

Two trials resulted: the first was declared a mistrial because of a reported juror bias, while the second found Abraham Rothschild innocent.

The details of the murder and subsequent trial are filled with the kind of folklore that still permeates the town today. Then and now, the people of Jefferson love a good story. They have painted in all the colorful details they could conjure up, ranging from the reputation and impropriety of the victim to questions of the purity and fairness of the jurors' decision. It is rumored, for example, that Bessie was pregnant when she was murdered, and a witness for Rothschild's defense claimed to have seen her with another man on two occasions before her Sunday picnic, once on Saturday and once on Thursday.

Some of the accounts would make good fireside ghost stories for Jodie Breckenridge's Friday night rendezvous at the Jefferson Hotel, for one rumor claims that all twelve jurors met violent deaths within the first year after the trial. Other stories claim that the verdict was not announced until after the train whistle blew, at which time twelve $1,000 bills were lowered into the room, presumably suspended from strings. Before Rothschild's arrest and trial, he was reported to have been in Cincinnati, where he stumbled drunk out into the street and attempted to shoot himself. What was intended as a fatal shot merely blinded one eye. The people of Jefferson use as proof of his guilt the visit of an elderly man with an eye patch in the 1890s. He allegedly asked to see Bessie's grave, knelt before it to say a prayer and placed roses there. A reenactment of the dramatic trial has become a pivotal part of the Jefferson historic Pilgrimage, performed every spring since 1955.

"Anyone seen Pup-pup?" an older man stuck his head in the side door of The Bakery.

"Oh he's probably under a table or something," our curly haired hostess replied, while stooping down to check.

Gulping iced tea, I lamented my scalded tongue. Needless to say, the catfish special was superior. Rick ordered a Sinful Brownie, the item that I'm sure Jefferson residents would argue puts The Bakery on the map. It was indeed a sinister-looking thing, a giant rectangle of a brownie piled high with what looked like layers of fudge frosting and marshmallow cream. One more for the road, and we were off. As we were leaving the restaurant, a pretty young girl in her early twenties popped her head in the front door and asked our hostess if she would be at tonight's game.

"Yep, I've got to cheer for both sides tonight because we're playin Joe's son's team, Charlie," she replied. I looked down at the sticker on the girl's shirt as I passed her in the doorway. "Hello My Name Is: Charlie" it read.

I walked outside to take a picture of the Jay Gould railroad car, and there was Pup-pup, leg hiked, passing his endorsement on the historical marker's signpost. We walked through the Excelsior House Hotel to take a few pictures before leaving town. The hotel has been continuously operating since the late 1850s. Host at one time to such famous guests as Lady Bird Johnson (whose name graces the Bridal Suite), Oscar Wilde, Ulysses S. Grant and Rutherford B. Hayes, the lobby of this opulent, antique-filled place contains a glass case with the original signatures of its famous historic guests. The courtyard, ballroom and dining room all parallel the lobby in their intricate collection of decorations, from hand-stitched tapestries and fragile lace to impenetrably timeless mahogany furniture. Back when the Excelsior House first opened, preceding the railroad, Jefferson was a town busy with travelers, as it was the westernmost port on the Red River, bringing cotton and other products from New Orleans and Shreveport into Texas.

Pup-pup.

A Jefferson Hotel horse.

We drove past the haunted Jefferson Hotel, where a driverless horse-drawn carriage waited patiently outside.

We've stopped for lunch and driven through countless Texas towns, but this one was particularly endearing to me. I could picture the townspeople's heads popping in and out of such spots as The Bakery when Diamond Bessie's body turned up under a drift of melting snow. I could picture the endless chain on which such rumors traveled and were invented and recycled, each time collecting more razzle-dazzle, but no one would be so brazen as to deny or even question their veracity. The town is even more endearing to me because the chain hasn't stopped yet. Like an electric current, it moves unbroken and unobstructed, the citizens of Jefferson kindling and regenerating it each spring at the Pilgrimage and every Friday night while they tiptoe, wide-eyed, carrying their lanterns and digital cameras. And it is endearing to me because the prettiest girl in town is named Charlie.

Out of Jefferson, the Forest Trail takes you, like a game of leapfrog, from Highway 49 to 805 to 43 and then back to 49. I can think of two reasons for this particular diversion from the straight and simple: the town of Karnack and Caddo Lake. The founders of Karnack evidently named their town because it was the same distance from Port Caddo as was the ancient Karnack, Egypt, from its capital, Thebes. In ancient Egypt, Thebes was the center of civil operations, while Karnack held the temples. The parallels here require a spark of one's imagination: Port Caddo served as the northeastern entry point for the Republic of Texas, and the Karnack of east Texas is the hometown of Lady Bird Johnson.

Caddo Lake is just a couple of miles northeast, and it bears the name of the Caddo Indians, who said that the lake had mystic origins. They believed that an earthquake created it, which was the result of the Great Spirit's anger at the disobedience of one of the Caddo chiefs. The more traditional theory is that the so-called Red River Raft, or a logjam, formed Caddo, one of the largest natural lakes in the South.

The short stint on Highway 805 is a chance for drivers to catch a glimpse of treasures more or less hidden. While one would argue that it makes more sense to stay on 49 to Marshall, the Forest Trail strays into uncharted territory every chance it gets. But who would want to miss the view that mixes lush fields covered with wildflowers and deep and dense piney woods? The wildflowers in Texas are a splendor to behold both for their abundance that comes very near profligacy and for the unique design of each single flower, shaped as a chalice of wine or a sombrero or colored like a woven tapestry. The deep scarlet of a thousand Indian paintbrushes set against a background of forest green would pique anyone's interest, but the startlingly enjoyable thing about looking at these little landscapes that Texas paints is that a twenty-foot-long section of these flowers is equally beautiful, but in a quite different way, to just one particular flower up close.

We followed Highway 49 into Marshall, passing along the way a Charolais cattle ranch advertising "Bulls for Sale." A Frenchman brought these long-bodied creamy white beeves to Mexico in the 1930s. The first to purchase France's white cows was the King Ranch, and the Charolais have since made their way into the Texas cattle industry for both beef and dairy. Perhaps because we rarely see them on our road trips, there's something rather feminine and sophisticated about the faces and soft-looking hide of these pure blond monsieurs and mademoiselles. Somehow I'm tempted to approach them at the fence with an extended hand and an *enchanté*!

As we entered Marshall, we immediately noticed a small restaurant that promised to be teeming with personality, Neely's BBQ—"Home of the Brown Pig" read the sign. It depicted a brown-skinned, round-bellied swine wearing an apron and a ruffled hat to match. This robust, smiling caricature no doubt draws Marshall residents and passersby in because she reminds them of the buxom, matronly figure depicted in old southern lore, one whose cooking could never be surpassed. I imagine many of those who now hold grandchildren and great-grandchildren in their arms hunger with nostalgia for those times when the conversation around the table and in the kitchen did not focus on the carbohydrate and fat content, using less salt or whether the fried chicken contains added hormones.

Marshall was a wealthy, prosperous town very early in its development, having the first telegraph in east Texas, which enabled the retrieval of the national news from New Orleans. It was also a bustling hub for traders and travelers to and from Louisiana. A roadside marker describes the old heavily traversed Marshall–Shreveport Stagecoach Road, which traced the same route we drove up Highway 43 to Jefferson:

> *In some areas, iron-rimmed wheels and horses' hooves trampled the narrow roadbed as much as 12 feet below the surrounding terrain. Travel over the dirt road was uncomfortable in dry weather and often impossible in rainy seasons. Regular stage service was established by 1850, with three arrivals and three departures weekly from Marshall. Arrival of the stage was a major event. At the sound of the driver's bugle, townspeople rushed to meet the incoming coach.*

Even though this region of northeast Texas saw early success and growth, of which this roadside marker bears evidence, it was also plagued for a short while by its location in what came to be known as the Neutral Zone. This area was disputed between Texas and Louisiana, and the ambiguity resulted in a lawless place that was attractive to criminals and corruption. Fort Crawford was built in 1839 near Hallsville to protect the settlers from the chaos. It served briefly as a fortress and refuge from Indians and outlaws. There are no ruins left of Fort Crawford today.

We came into Longview on Highway 80, and there was a huge mess of rush-hour traffic. Following the map on our Forest Trails brochure, we turned south on Highway 31, where construction slowed us down for four miles until we reached Kilgore, arguably the most famous town in east Texas. The discovery of oil in the 1930s brought Kilgore both the fame and the rowdiness that frequently accompanies wealth. When the oil boom reached its peak, there were over 1,100 wells inside the city limits. One of these was reportedly drilled through the terrazzo floor of the Kilgore National Bank. There is a park in Kilgore today where replicated oil derricks signify what was at one time "the world's richest acre." A marker in the park gives the staggering dimensions for the size and extent of Kilgore's rags-to-riches story:

> *Part of fabulous East Texas oil field discovered in 1930. This 1.195-acre tract had first production on June 17, 1937, when the Mrs. Bess Johnson–Adams & Hale No. 1 well was brought in. Developed before well-spacing rules, this block is the most densely drilled tract in the world, with 24 wells on 10 lots owned by six different operators. This acre has produced over two and a half million barrels of crude oil; selling at $1.10 to $3.25 a barrel, it has brought more than five and a half million dollars. A forest of steel derricks for many years stood over the more than 1,000 wells in downtown Kilgore, marking the greatest concentration of oil wells in the history of the world. Dozens of these derricks still dot the city's internationally famous skyline. Since 1930, the East Texas oil field has produced nearly four billion barrels of oil. It now has more than 17,000 producing wells, and geologists predict a future of at least 45 years for this "granddaddy of oil fields."*

This quiet little town could never have prepared for the kind of population growth it saw once the oil began to flow, multiplying precipitously from seven hundred to ten thousand barrels in just the first three days after the discovery. The Texas Rangers sent "Lone Wolf" Gonzaullas to Kilgore to single-handedly police the town and keep the gangsters and crooks in line. A 2003 editorial in Longview's online news journal describes Lone Wolf's role in restoring some semblance of order to a town that was starting to become familiar with mob rule:

> *Chaos ruled the day when Gonzaullas arrived in Gregg County. In August 1931, Texas Gov. Ross Sterling declared martial law in the oil*

field and sent in 1,300 National Guardsmen plus several Rangers to restore order. Only a village when oil was found, Kilgore had been too tiny to have its own jail. So Gonzaullas solved the problem by marching his criminals down to a local abandoned church where a long chain had been strung from one interior wall to another. There the unlucky fellows were bound to smaller trace chains connected to the big chain. The contraption came to be called "Lone Wolfs Trotline," and it was an experience to be avoided.

Gonzaullas effectively eliminated much of the pervasive criminal element in Kilgore and reduced the amount of "hot" oil being exported at the time. His reputation traveled throughout Texas and all the way south to the Rio Grande, where he was known as El Lobo Solo.

Leaving Gonzaullas's jurisdiction behind, we took Highway 42 through the towns of New London and Price at the time of day when the sun is low in the western sky and shines horizontally through the towering trees that line the road. This kind of light has visible razor edges slicing through hard pine, and it reminds me of the technique used in films to signify the appearance of an angel or some supernatural being, just beyond the woods and past the realm of total visibility.

We left the pines to their spirits as we entered New London, which like many small towns in east Texas witnessed a shift from the manual labor of farming to the labor required to implement and maintain an oil field. For many landowners, wealth accompanied this shift. However, the auspices of the oil boom were darkened dramatically by another kind of boom when the expensive steel-framed school building, which New London's windfall of oil money could finally afford, exploded in 1937. A teacher turned on a sanding machine in a closed space that was filled with undetectable gas, and nearly three hundred people were killed. The force of the explosion threw a two-ton piece of concrete twenty feet, where it crushed a car. At the time, this event was certainly the biggest school accident in U.S. history. There is a museum in town that memorializes the tragic story through pictures and firsthand accounts.

The Forest Trail continues on Highway 42 south to 839, which runs past Lake Striker and is to me part of the most beautiful section of the drive. This road is secluded and hilly, so that each time you climb to the top of a hill, the next portrait of landscape appears like a pleasant surprise. It's difficult to keep up with all of the road changes on this route, but it is certainly worth the trouble. From 839, you take Highway 84 east and then south again on 225. Whether or not it was intentional I have no idea, but this segment of the trip is such a smart contrast to the previous feeling created by the steady, stoic evergreens that rose high above your vehicle on both sides of the road. They are picturesque in their resilience, abundance and repetition. Like the evenly metered rhyming lines of a Robert Frost poem, the "piney woods" segments of the drive engage us for their familiarity:

> *The woods are lovely, dark and deep,*
> *But I have promises to keep*
> *And miles to go before I sleep,*
> *And miles to go before I sleep.*

So on we go, discovering an entirely new view. On 225, the horizon rolls like a turbulent ocean made up of a hundred far-off hills. Abandoning the repeated rhyme and rhythm we have come to expect, this region offers the randomness of land that is not flat, and its hills extend on all sides as far as the eye can see. We crossed the Nacogdoches County line, zigged and zagged our way through Cushing, population 647, where we passed the Burgers N Bull restaurant and dashed quickly through Looeyville, undetected I believe. Highway 343 took us into Nacogdoches.

A legend explains the connected origins of Nacogdoches, Texas, and Natchitoches, Louisiana (the latter pronounced NACK-a-dish). According to the old story, a Caddo Indian chief who lived along the Sabine River sent his twin sons off in opposite directions to prove themselves as leaders and establish their own tribes. Nacogdoches was the brother who ventured west into the setting sun, and Natchitoches went east into the rising sun. From ancient times, it has been told, these towns flourished as twin brothers would, and they remained filially connected by one of the oldest roads in the United States, El Camino Real.

In 1716, the Spanish established a mission in Nacogdoches, which was led by Father Antonio Margil, whose *ojos*, or eyes, became another facet of the legends surrounding the oldest town in Texas. A year after the Mission of Our Lady of Guadalupe was built, the region saw a severe drought. The Indians suffered terribly, as they could not sustain their crops. A roadside marker at the La Nana Creek Bridge tells what happened when "Los Ojos de Padre Margil" became famous:

> *In the summer of 1718, according to tradition, Father Margil was led by a vision to a point near this site where the bed of La Nana Creek made a sharp bend. There he struck the overhanging rock shelf with his staff, and a stream of water gushed forth. Some accounts say that he made two openings in the rock, which became known as "The Eyes of Father Margil." This miraculous event inspired the Indians, and a relief expedition later found conditions at the mission greatly improved. In 1720, Father Margil founded Mission San Jose y San Miguel de Aguayo in San Antonio. He died in Mexico City. "The Holy Spring," now dry except during very rainy weather, symbolizes the faith and endurance of the Spanish missionaries.*

In 1772, the Spanish decided to abandon the mission and move all the Nacogdoches settlers to San Antonio. But, like its namesake, the twin brother who traveled westward toward the sunset, Nacogdoches was destined to survive. In 1779, Antonio Gil Y'Barbo initiated a trip back from San Antonio, and several settlers joined him. He built a stone house right in the center of town, which in this early time was the intersection of the only two existing roads, El Camino Real and El Calle del Norte. Y'Barbo's house came to be called Old Stone Fort, and it witnessed the forefront of Texas's revolutionary history, serving at various times as "trading post, store, warehouse, town hall, fort, barracks, church, tavern, and saloon," according to the historical marker's description. Today there is a museum at the Old Stone Fort.

Even though, like a hypnotist putting his patient into a trance, the Forest Trail beckoned us to follow five more intriguing swings of the pendulum, we took Highway 59 from Nacogdoches straight into Houston. We had no daylight left, and there were miles to go before I would sleep, miles to go before I would sleep.

Forest Trail West

After exploring east Texas in April, Rick and I were certain we had to see the other half of the Forest Trail. So in the hundred-degree days of July, when slimy stumps reared their ugly heads above the water in our unnaturally shallow, evaporating lakes and when you could easily fry an egg on the hood of the car, we sought shade in the form of the east Texas pines. Once again it took at least two hours to get far enough east on I-30 to enter the route. We've all learned in life that timing is everything, and we timed our crossing of Lake Ray Hubbard perfectly. A vibrant, low eastern sun was there to greet us, spreading its glow over the water, which was tricked out with gold sparkles. Here, just east of Dallas, was a nightclub diva, fresh as the start of her night, first thing in the morning.

Road trips bring you through so many towns and past so many signs that it's hard to keep the eyes tuned in and keenly waiting for the one that's going to matter. It takes some practice to actually stare out the window and look at things rather than just to watch the blur of brush along the side of the road pass by while thinking of grocery lists and upcoming birthdays. I guess for me it's just a matter of getting into the car with a certain attitude about the trip. You have to believe that you haven't seen it all before: the cows, the churches, the Cracker Barrels and the dilapidated barns. You may have seen them already. You may have driven east on I-30 to Sulphur Springs twenty times, but the attitude it takes is that you haven't seen them on this particular day when, for example, the sun is feeling particularly flirty. Anyway, we've passed thousands of city limit signs, some with population counts, some without, but the last time we did the Forest Trail, I completely missed one sign in particular. And the moment I saw it, I immediately cleared my head of checkbook registers and to-do lists, for on this day we were driving through the city limits of Fate.

The Sulphur Springs exit was our turnoff from I-30, and just a few moments on Highway 154 brought us to Highway 11, where we went south in an eastward swing. This route, just like its pendulous eastern half, literally makes giant "S" shapes all the way down to Houston. Southeastward on 11 is pretty—bucolic, really. The unnaturally silent town of Martin Springs, which is too tiny to appear on the map, consisted of a cemetery, a Baptist church and a few Holsteins grazing. During the few minutes it took us to drive through, the population was zero. South of Winnsboro, Highway 312 was just as quiet. We coasted along a shaded two-lane road while my eyes fixed on the tilting glide of three buzzards overhead. To me, buzzards are graceful and nearly majestic, until you see them up close.

It didn't surprise me, then, that we missed our turn onto 2088 after spotting a small deer crossing the road in long, graceful leaps. Last year, during "the season," I got up on a freezing cold morning, before dawn, to sit in a deer stand with my husband and watch them move, as they are prone to do just before daylight, through the woods in the security of the darkness. Once my eyes were acclimated, I watched and watched. I saw birds, a noisy hog the color of dirt that didn't appear to have a schedule to keep, more birds and scads of ladybugs but no deer. It was explained to me in a barely audible whisper, while I shivered and watched, that when they do appear, if in fact they do, it's like magic. You just blink and one's there. Just as the sun was coming up, just before it was time to pack the whole thing up and call it quits, I glanced at a tree on the edge of the woods and then down at my gloves, where another ladybug had landed, then back; in that second's time, there was a young buck, frozen as a sculpture, listening, as if he'd been there for moments already. So it's a treasure to me to see these little roadside spirits, but forget about reaching for the camera. Like the ghost at the Jefferson Hotel, they probably only show up on a digital but disappear when you make prints. The pines are full of these pleasant little surprises, making it worth the trouble to take so many different roads.

In order to stick with the route laid out on the brochure, we turned onto Highway 154, where we saw another deer—a tiny fawn with white spots—in Little Hope. Even though the area was settled in the 1850s, presumably the town's name appeared later with the establishment of the Little Hope Missionary Baptist Church. The community had little hope that the church would last past its first year.

On Highway 154, we headed into Quitman, where we stopped to take a picture of the Wood County Courthouse. I don't know which they are more proud of here in Quitman: being the birthplace of Sissy Spacek or hosting the Governor Hogg Shrine. There's a marker describing James Stephen Hogg at the courthouse, and then the Hogg Historic Park has museums, a honeymoon cottage and hiking trails for the more modern of visitors. Texans want to commemorate Hogg's life because he was the first state governor who was native-born. Hogg wanted to squelch corruption in the business and political sectors—namely, I think, when these two paths crossed—and he was known for his outspoken charisma, ending one speech with the entreaty, "Let us have Texas, the Empire State, governed by the people; not Texas, the truck-patch, ruled by corporate lobbyists." Hogg's connections with the town of Quitman, however, preceded fiery speeches and his term as governor. He worked for the local newspapers, there and in Tyler; he served a couple of years as justice of the peace; and he aided the sheriff, for which he caught hell on at least one occasion. More specifically, he caught a beating and a gunshot in the back. He recovered from this wound, and he went on to become one of the biggest names in Texas politics.

After Quitman, we headed south on 37, which turns into 69 in Mineola (called Sodom until the 1870s). We continued to curve southward into Lindale, and I spotted a giant welcome sign for the city of Good Country Living, which was half buried in tall grass. Good country living, indeed. From there, the map carries you east on 16 toward Red Springs and then drops you south on 14 into Tyler. Along Highway 14, we passed the Tiger Creek Wildlife Refuge, which is a rescue compound for big cats. Set on twenty-five acres of land, the refuge is home to about thirty-five cats. Tiger Creek has had national attention since Animal Planet filmed *Growing Up Tiger* on the premises in 2002, featuring the first year of development for two cubs, Sarge and Lily. Animal Planet still shows the program occasionally, each time giving the whole world a glance at one shady little patch of east Texas.

Getting through Tyler mid-morning had its potential snags, so we caught the loop and circled the city instead of cutting right through the center, as the Forest Trail brochure would have us do. After all, there were plenty of miles to cover in a day's time. Arguably east Texas's busiest city, Tyler's modern moniker is the nation's Rose Capital, and it's been known as such for quite a while. Peaches were the original cash crop of Smith County until blight obliterated the orchards. Most of the peach growers switched to roses, and by the Roaring Twenties, there were literally millions of rose bushes blooming in the area. The first Tyler Rose Festival was held in 1933. Even in Fort Worth, you'll often pass a side-of-the-road vendor with "Tyler Roses" painted on a plywood sign. I attended a wedding at the Tyler Rose Garden once, and it felt like I was in the center of an endless maze of very neatly pruned hedges. These were nothing like the burly, wayward bushes in my yard that grow every way except neatly along the trellis I've provided. And no mythic Minotaur awaited within these thick, thorny walls, just the evidence of many a ghost of weddings past.

The city of Tyler has all kinds of ghosts in its history, starting with the Caddo tribes who owned the land first, hundreds of years before its first glimpse by European eyes. The Neches River that runs alongside our driving route for a good many miles also carries the legacy of east Texas's natives, for it bears the name of one southern Caddo tribe. If nothing else, we owe a great debt to the Caddos for the name of our state—their term for "friend" was *Tejas*. The Caddos first saw Europeans in 1542 when the Hernando de Soto Expedition passed through. The next European to befriend the Caddos was a missionary from Spain, Jose Francisco Calahorra y Saenz, but the more famous visit to the area was when Pedro Vial and Francisco Xavier Fragoso passed through the region heading from Santa Fe to Natchitoches, Louisiana. They forged the Vial-Fragoso trail (there is a roadside marker describing the route just six miles north of Lindale). The few months it took them to blaze this trail in 1788 became more valuable than these two tenacious men could ever have suspected. The first footprints they made would later be followed by others, over and over again, to drive cattle. The thousands of hooves that were obliged to shuffle and stamp their way across the Vial-Fragoso did a primitive but effective job of paving a road the stagecoaches could then use. Eventually, the trail became the Dallas–Shreveport Road, all beginning with the curiosity and diligence of a two-man partnership.

The Tyler area wasn't always the peaceful, rosy place we now know. In 1862, Camp Ford, a post to be used as a training camp for enlistees, was built just outside of town. Just a year later, though, the Confederates transformed it into a prison camp to hold Union POWs. When just a few prisoners camped there, they were responsible for putting up their own shelter out in the open range, with ample guard to keep watch. They did everything from using blankets as tents to building the popular "shebang," which was little more than a carved-out hillside with an A-framed entrance.

As the number of Union captives increased, slave labor was used to build a sixteen-foot-high stockade enclosing the few acres of camp. Rations were a pint of cornmeal and a pound of beef each day, but as the number of prisoners increased, they often received just a quarter of this quantity. Many of the prisoners never saw a change of clothing. As many as six thousand total prisoners were kept at Camp Ford for some time during its short, two-year existence.

Reconstruction brought with it the dismantling of Camp Ford and the sour conditions that existed there, but a climate of fierce racial tension prevailed long after those sixteen-foot walls came down. In fact, an official with the Freedmen's Bureau, headquartered in Tyler, used the phrase "reign of terror" to describe the white hostility that ensued when the agency attempted such initiatives as education and voting rights for the blacks of Smith County.

There were shootouts; one trial in 1871 unraveled into mayhem when the parties involved left the courtroom and took to the streets with guns blazing. And in 1874, the already blood-splattered roadways of Tyler witnessed a lynching. Our twenty-first-century eyes see all types of grisly violence: the sociopath, armed with a chainsaw, chasing terrified coeds; the vengeance-crazed gangster who opens fire on a cozy, dimly lit Italian restaurant, killing twelve people just to hit one mark; and the surveillance camera footage on the evening news of a burglar smashing a full liter of Smirnoff over a liquor store cashier's head. However common these images are to us when delivered from behind the ubiquitous glass screen, though, I can't quite get my mind around the reality of a mob lynching or a shootout right in the middle of downtown Tyler, especially while we make our way south on Loop 323 on a sunny Saturday morning. There is unison here. There's good Mexican food. There are roses for sale.

Highway 155 branches off the southwest end of the loop, and it's one of the few true straight lines we followed that day. We drove through Noonday, population 515, where the Noonday onion grows. It's one of the sweetest there is, and an onion has to be grown within ten miles of the town to be considered a Noonday. The town didn't even get a dot on the state map I was using, but it sure did make its existence known as we passed through by car. I noticed an operating farmers' market (you see plenty of abandoned flea markets in tiny Texas town sites, with nothing left but the sign out by the road and, occasionally, the framework of some of the stalls). But Noonday's market was up and running, and onions, I imagine, were the order of the day; I also noticed a whole lot of rocking chairs for sale. I'm betting these are handmade, and it would be worth the two hours out here from Dallas sometime to find out.

Our straight line southwestward carried us across Lake Palestine, whose waters that day were a little depleted by the heat, just like our lakes at home. It's a grand, wide view, though, since the lake has a long and narrow shape and 155 slices diagonally through the bottom half of it. Then, as quickly as we passed through Noonday, we left behind us Coffee City and Berryville, two little settlements right on the lake. We stopped for lunch in Frankston, where Frank Beard, ZZ Top's only beardless band member, was born.

It was just after noon as we rolled up to the Country Kettle Buffet, and it warrants emphasis here that Rick and I stick to a strict no-buffet dining policy when we're on the road together. For reasons that need no further elaboration here, I'm reluctant to touch the handle of a pair of salad tongs that fifty other hands have touched, and I'm even more reluctant to eat food that's been sitting out on a steam table so long that only what's scorched and welded to the very bottom of the pan is actually at a safe temperature for bacteria-free consumption. So we entered the Kettle "just to see" what it was all about and maybe to order a couple of glasses of tea first. At once, I noticed the kitschy décor of the countrified home, like the wooden placard, with two bowed legs punctuated at the ends with a pair of brown boots, reading "Don't squat with yer spurs on," also the title of a well-known book of cowboy humor. Then there was the ever-loved and overused "I was country when country wasn't cool." Maybe these silly phrases make people smile not because they are original but because they are so familiar. Anyway, I scanned the room until it seemed like the appropriate time had elapsed for Rick and me to appraise the buffet. There were hoards of others there eating—always a good cue to follow. And every food offering had visible steam rising off of it, so we shrugged our shoulders, grabbed a couple of plates and threw caution to the wind.

With full stomachs, we got back on the Forest Trail, passing Frankston's Church of Christ, where the sign that day read "When love is divided it is multiplied." But when this area was first settled, it was land being divided, not love, and what multiplied exponentially was the bitter rage the area's tribes, mostly the Cherokees, felt as a result of their disenfranchisement. This area between Tyler and Palestine that we traversed next is the basic location for the violent events that started the Cherokee War, which occurred between the Texans and a few tribes, not just Cherokees, who were in alliance with and incited to action by Mexican rebel Vicente Cordova, who believed that collaborating with the Indians would make easier a later invasion of Texas by the Mexican army. The Cherokees, feeling like Sam Houston failed them in his promises to keep peace with the tribe, had previously inhabited parts of east Texas and held quite a bitter and justifiable grudge. The Republic of Texas Senate rescinded Houston's treaty that guaranteed them possession of their land. The senate coldly determined instead that the Cherokees had no rights under Texas law, and the land was divvied up among the whites accordingly.

In the biggest of all depredations on the east Texas frontier, the Killough family bore the brunt of the natives' rage. This family unfortunately settled on a part of the tract of land that Houston had originally deeded to the Cherokees in 1836. Catching wind of Cordova's Rebellion, thirty of the members of the Killough settlement sought refuge in Nacogdoches, but the Cherokees did not mind postponing their vengeance until the whites returned in the fall. When they attacked in early October 1838, a total of eighteen white settlers were either murdered or captured, making this single attack bigger in scope than the more famous attack on Parker's Fort. What's also significant about the Killough massacre is that it served as the catalyst for Rusk's organizing a militia and inciting the Cherokee War.

General Rusk led about 200 men into the Kickapoo Village, which was literally just two and a half miles south of Frankston, where we ate lunch. The warriors they fought there were a combination of Caddos, Biloxies, Coushattas and Cherokees, with a few Mexican rebels, totaling about 250. After some bloody fighting, Rusk's forces routed them, causing them to leave 11 bodies of their fallen warriors on the field. The Indians suffered approximately 70 wounded or killed, while the Texans estimated a mere 12 wounded and 35 horses slain. Now called the Kickapoo War, Rusk's 1838 fight preceded the Cherokee War's most decisive battle, the Battle of the Neches, which occurred in July of the following year.

After the Killough massacre, and the Kickapoo War that followed, the Republic of Texas's newly elected president, General Mirabeau Lamar, decided that the Indians must be driven out of the country. In a speech he made as new president of the republic, demonstrating that he was the polar opposite of the once sympathetic Sam Houston, Lamar indicated vehemently that the "proper policy to be pursued toward the barbarian race is absolute expulsion from the country...Our only security against a savage foe is to allow no security to him." Thus, Lamar ordered several of his commanders to combine their forces in proximity to Cherokee territory, so Burleson, Rusk and Landrum rendezvoused and consolidated their troops to be commanded by General Kelsey H. Douglass.

From atop distant hills and under the thick cover of tall, wooly pines, the Indians watched the operations of this military force carefully, and they readily gave them the battle they were seeking. After fierce fighting just east of Tyler, on the north end of present-day Lake Palestine, the five hundred Texans defeated eight hundred Cherokee allies, killing their leader, eighty-three-year-old Chief Bowles. Most accounts of the Battle of the Neches commend Bowles's great bravery. His body remained on the Neches battlefield for several years, soon reduced to just a skull and bones. There were about one hundred other casualties, including another Cherokee leader, Chief Big Mush. Those Indians who remained, defeated and mourning the loss of their warriors, began their retreat into Oklahoma, leaving their prized east Texas land to the whites.

First divided...then multiplied.

Outside of Frankston, you have to briefly imagine these ghosts of the past for scenery, because a short jog west on 175 shows you absolutely nothing but shaggy fields all the way out to the horizon. In Poynor, we turned back to the south on 315; I noticed a country store and café at the corner with literally piles and piles of stuff outside. It was a jarring transition from the smooth blur of fields that my eyes had scanned for ten miles. But the view that followed atoned beautifully for this unfortunate little eyesore. Highway 315 is hilly, with some sections deeply shaded and others starkly lighted, creating a camouflage palette in forty shades of green. Here was no ordinary tableau, monochromatic though it was. It was like looking at a giant, swirling, ocean-like collage inspired by varied hues of asparagus, limes, olives and even speckled pears, with rich pine needles arbitrarily thrown into the mix. To me, there's nothing prettier than the accidental art that occurs in nature. And to follow the scene of forty shades, the piney woods could be nothing less than extraordinary, and so they were. Giant and wide, pines towered lazily over us like wooly mammoths on both sides of the road, allowing just a skinny strip of sky to peek through right above the car. Just after we crossed Brushy Creek, for a bit of contrast, throw in a few trees with fern-like leaves and dainty pink feathery blossoms at the feet of these giants. Each of these looked like a showgirl's boa. What splendor.

What soon follows on the Forest route is a continuation of this area that is thicker with bloody skirmishes between the Indians and the frontier folks than any other on this trip; first, though, another quick westward jog, on 321 to Montalba, before dropping down on Highway 19 into Palestine. When we spotted a corrugated metal shed with a sentimental collection of meticulously placed road signs covering its side, we slowed down for some pictures of this town. With the largest circle filling the angle formed by the roof, and every other shape seeming to fit just perfectly where it was placed, from rectangular "One Way" to the X-shaped railroad crossing, it was like pop art meets junk collector, in another unexpectedly tiny shaded patch of east Texas. We also photographed Montalba's little downtown block that preserves its origins, a wooden storefront jail adjacent to a bank, before driving into the region where our Indian attacks occurred.

Just two miles west of Palestine, a ranger company built a blockhouse, partnered by the settlers who built a stockade, on an acre of the town site of Houston in May 1836. It's hard to believe that the sprawling city of Houston that we know today had Anderson County here in the east Texas

A Gulf shed along the Forest route.

pines as its original prospective location. After the town was abandoned, and Anderson's county seat moved to Palestine, the structure took on the name Fort Houston. When white expansion pressed westward into Texas, the Indians felt the squeeze, and they answered back with tactics that should have terrorized these folks right back to Carolina and Tennessee and wherever else they came from. I can imagine the frustration and complete shock the Caddo and Cherokee tribes expressed at their fireside councils when their vicious attacks brought more whites onto their land and not less.

The white settlers didn't run back east. In fact, after the attacks, they appealed immediately to Sam Houston for more force, which came from Fort Jesup in the form of a nine-hundred-pound cannon to add a bit of fire to the breath of the dragon that they imagined would protect them and their humble Fort Houston in the center of town. I don't think these eastern tribes could have imagined in their wildest dreams that these simple folks—after seeing their siblings' scalps razed clean off, their mothers and grandmothers stripped of their dresses and sadistically abused, their fathers' limbs pierced through with gunshot and, after all of these things, their houses ransacked and beds sliced open to send a flurry of feathers showering down and settling finally in sticky pools of fresh blood on the floors of their houses—would be so resolute in their desire to stay and that they would have the backing of a forcefully well-equipped and well-trained militia. I imagine that they continued to be astounded every time they had to fight the whites again for land they had actually owned for thousands of years and that they were astounded all the way through the Cherokee War and on into their final, tragic retreat into Oklahoma.

In the Houston town site, the actual fort was never attacked by Indians, but the surrounding settlers whom it was supposed to protect saw more than their fair share of hostilities from area tribes. Even the Texas Rangers, whenever they left the blockhouse walls, faced danger. In January 1837, a party of six rangers headed out toward the Trinity River to find hogs gone astray. When two went back for a canoe, a band of warriors descended on the four who remained. Three of these men, Columbus Anderson and two named Faulkenberry, a father and son, were severely wounded but reportedly swam heroic lengths of the Trinity before finally being forced to succumb to their wounds. Reports say that Anderson swam a ways and then also crawled a whole two miles before his death. The fourth man made it back to the fort alive, although his thigh had been ripped open by a bullet.

Just a few months later, Daniel McLean and his brother-in-law were killed when they set out to retrieve stolen horses. McLean was one of the original three hundred to settle in Texas and a skilled Indian fighter. In an ominously prescient letter to his son back in January just a day before the Anderson-Faulkenberry deaths occurred, he wrote of the stolen horses and of the imminent invasion of Texas by Mexican troops. Also in the letter, he said of the Indians, "We may suppose that at the rise of the grass they will be on all sides," and unfortunately, in his case, they were.

Two years after McLean's death, a widow and her children who lived near Fort Houston also suffered the fierce wrath of natives scorned. A band of fifteen appeared at her homestead one night, just a couple of weeks after her husband, Charles Campbell, had died. She was able to get two of her five children, one seventeen and one four years old, hidden under the floorboards of the house before the Indians broke through the door, chopping into Mrs. Campbell's arm with a tomahawk. They quickly killed her, along with her fourteen-year-old and eleven-year-old children. The only ones to survive were the two concealed under the house and a slave whose life the Indians graciously spared. They understood, it seems, the difference between the white property owners and the slaves they would encounter at these homesteads. These tribes were perceptive enough to notice that blacks were no more in control of the when and the where of white settlement than they themselves were.

The loop we made around Palestine showed no evidence of its bloodier, early times. In 2003, debris from the explosion of the space shuttle *Columbia* showered down on parts of this land. Now it is back to the status quo, and busy streets and dogwoods abound. The next part of our route was a series of turnoffs that headed southeastward along farm roads, passing areas with houses sweetly secluded. In places like this, I know why the real estate world uses catchy phrases like "well appointed." We wove our way, using the trail brochure as our guide, through Slocum and Denson Springs.

The next part of the drive is another of the route's rebellious romps northeast and then southeast and then all the way back to the west, bringing you back to the very road on which this giant diversion began. But they're justified in doing this to motorists because this little time-consuming jaunt makes a deep crescent shape into the thick of the Davy Crockett National Forest. What the heck, right? We'd eaten lunch and the sun was out.

The Neches River forms the eastern edge of the 162,000-acre forest, which lies mostly in Houston County. Basically, the first arc of the crescent takes Highway 227, and the second half, Highway 7. Historical markers dotted our way, signifying mostly old community names and family cemeteries. This trip through the Crockett forest is an alluring, shaded and curvy path. Here the pines are long and lean, unlike their humped and wooly counterparts farther back. Like a larger-than-life gospel choir they reach high upward and lightly sway in worship of sun and breeze, occasionally reaching across the road toward one another.

After the turn westward on Highway 7, passing by the Ratcliff Lake area, we stopped to snap a picture or two of the town of Kennard's roadside marker. For a population of only three hundred, the folks here have outdone themselves to welcome drivers and tout their pride in their

The Kennard Tiger mascot.

home team's mascot, the Tiger. We were impressed with monuments they'd set up here, and to see what the people were like, we photographed a few of the homesteads we passed on our way through. Here they are in the thick of the forest, yet the Kennardans have set out to differentiate their tiny town from all the others. I'm wondering if they put together this Tiger and Crockett shrine after getting word that drivers following the Forest Trail brochure would be swinging through these trees. Plus, they know they've got to compete with that grand choir of pines. Alleluia; go, fight, win.

After this brief interlude, which was one of my favorites on this trip, we emerged out of the forest and headed straight into the town of Crockett, "Paradise in the Pines" and Houston County's seat. Of course, the town's settlers named it after David Crockett, who was reportedly a neighbor of theirs back home in Tennessee. Legend has it that Davy Crockett camped in the area on his way down to San Antonio to fight at the Alamo. In the town's early years, Crockett whites suffered the wrath of Cherokee and Alabama-Coushatta warriors, so their log courthouse doubled as a fort, where the citizens sought refuge when they had any advance notice of Indian attacks. The courthouse standing there today is shaded by a gorgeous, enormous magnolia, whose glossy leaves reflect rays of sunlight here and there like a watch face doing the characteristic tilts and turns of friendly conversation.

From Crockett, the Forest Trail resumes its standard "S" shape, serpent-like, soporific, down Highway 19, sweeping across I-45 to catch Huntsville and pass Sam Houston's grave. The city is probably best known today for the Texas State Penitentiary, which got its first inmate on October 1, 1849. (The first convicts to do time here were a cattle thief, a horse thief and a murderer.) In fact, I've never driven through Huntsville without checking the door locks and watching the shoulders on either side of the road for hitchhikers wearing conspicuous orange coveralls. You never know.

An impressive sixty-six-foot statue of Sam Houston awaits drivers on the side of I-45 in Huntsville, where he spent the last years of his life. Houston's life was quite a saga, beginning in his mid-childhood years when he retreated to the woods to keep company with the Cherokee boys he had befriended. As the story goes, he took Homer's *Iliad* with him out there to read by the light of the Indians' fire. He spent most of his time in the woods with the tribe until he was eighteen, and then he taught school awhile before joining the army as a common enlistee, something that lessened his esteem among his peers, who already undoubtedly thought his fraternizing with the natives odd, to say the least.

By the time Houston entered law school in Tennessee at the age of twenty-six, he had already fought the famous Tohopeka Battle (the

Battle of the Horseshoe), winning the admiration of Andrew Jackson for his courage. He had to threaten to run a comrade through with his sword in order to get him to rip an arrowhead out of his thigh, and he survived this and many other severe wounds at Tohopeka. Houston soon became a well-loved politician and was elected governor of Tennessee. Just before he would surely have been reelected to a second term, he snuck away in disguise to rejoin his Cherokee friends, namely the chief Oolooteekah (John Jolly), who had adopted him as a son when he was a boy. The people in Tennessee were confused at this sudden and stealthy exit from office, but not the chief, who said that "eleven winters" had passed since he had seen his son, and he knew the Great Spirit would bring him back when the tribe was in trouble. They were indeed in trouble, for the whites were quickly running them out of their land. Houston appealed to President Jackson, his old commanding officer, who enthusiastically received him and agreed to pay the tribes for their land. Apparently, Jackson is the reason Houston came to Texas, for at this conference the president commissioned him to go there and work on "the Comanche problem."

Houston made quite a name for himself in Texas; he's arguably the most famous name there is, rivaled perhaps only by Stephen F. Austin. He was commander in chief of the Texas army while it fought for independence from Mexico, twice a president of the republic, a state senator when it became a state and a governor. There could be a monument to Houston's legacy in nearly every region of Texas, but Huntsville is where he retired and eventually died; it is rumored that his last words were "Texas, Margaret, Texas."

The Forest Trail creates the bottom half of our inverted "S" shape by taking 1791 out west and dropping down into a small chunk of the Sam Houston National Forest, just west of Lake Conroe. Inside the forest, we cruised past horse farms, which always look like such peaceful places to me, and headed due south to Montgomery. An old fashioned–looking town of fewer than five hundred people, Montgomery has a Pioneer Museum we snapped a few photos of, just to admire their preservation of the way things used to look. Highway 105 brought us back around eastward to Conroe, and from there it means, unfortunately nowadays, that you'll be crawling along in traffic for some thirty miles until Houston.

Making this drive gave me a new respect for east Texas, for until my travels with Rick I had always heard things like, "There's nothing out there past Dallas but Shreveport." I love this region we drove through; it's cool and shady, slow-paced, breezy, tall and proud. There's something else, too, about east Texas that we would do well to think about once in a while, when they implode a historic downtown building to replace it with new fashionable urban lofts and when the days of heat over one hundred degrees exceed the number of home games the Kennard Tigers have won. There's something else: evergreens are trustworthy.

Highway 6 Trail

When I lived in Dallas, I always took I-45 down to Houston. I watched as the Woodlands area exploded, and eventually Conroe's city limits also became indistinguishable from the oozing urban monster directly south of it. With growth comes tax revenue, and with tax revenue comes road construction, and what follows is the evil of all evils for those among us who are short on patience: traffic. I came to dread the drive, which at first was an easy three-and-a-half-hour shot. I also eventually moved to Fort Worth, and I soon discovered the panacea for all things evil: Highway 6.

I've since gone down it and up it many, many times, and that's the route Rick chose for our homeward trip in July, after we headed down to Houston, tracing the western side of the Forest Trail. That morning we took 290 west to Hempstead. There are a number of ways to get out of Houston—the quicker the better in my opinion. Don't get me wrong; there are a number of good reasons to be in Houston, but the traffic on the major thoroughfares is not one of them. Once you get on the road, you've got to get the hell out of town. I like taking I-10 west to Brookshire and heading north on Farm Road 359 to pick up 6. But on this day, we had buckets of rain, and 290 happened to be the swiftest escape route.

Driving cautiously through Bellville and Navasota, we were subdued into silence and keen concentration while the windshield wipers strenuously sloshed sheets of rain back and forth. It was the kind of storm that hammers loudly on every surface of the car and also the kind of storm that floods Houston's streets in the blink of an eye. Gladly, we had pushed off in time.

Highway 6 cuts through the College Station area, passing by Texas A&M, which opened in 1876, the first public institution of higher learning in the state. As its name pretty clearly indicates, it's a college town and was named the most educated city in Texas in 2006 by *Money* magazine. But education isn't what shows itself most ostensibly to people passing through. It's the charm, the downright chivalrous nature of the people (mostly former and present Aggies) you'll encounter when you drive up 6 through the area. My mother went to College Station from Houston a while back for a day trip to the George Bush Library, and she got disoriented trying to get back to the highway and head home. She pulled up alongside a pickup with a few young men in it and asked them to please just point her in the direction of the highway. Their reply (and she still talks about this one for its remarkable contrast to the hostility you encounter daily from Houston motorists) was: "No, ma'am. We'll *show* you." The boys then drove in front of her, and in a few U-turns they got her back onto 6 southbound for home. It seems like there's an unwritten code out there in the heart of the Brazos Valley that all the residents tacitly follow, and it sure sets them apart.

Mid-morning brought us plunging headlong into the rain and a sea of courteous drivers, but we knew eventually that we'd get far enough north of it. The sun did come out, in Hearne, the Sunflower Capital of Texas. People there have seen their share of rain. Just a few months before this drive, Hearne had seventeen inches in one hour, causing heavy floods. The town is most noted in history for two things. The first is the historic railroad depot, which is right on Highway 6, though it's been moved across the road from its original location. There are plans in the works to create a museum out of it. The second is Camp Hearne, a POW camp that housed mostly German prisoners of World War II. Under the Geneva Convention, the POWs could not be forced to work, so they held classes, played sports, watched movies and, because the Germans housed at the camp were mainly part of the Afrika Korps from Tunisia, enjoyed concerts. The troops were brought to Hearne with all of their orchestra instruments in tow. Camp Hearne operated for a couple of years, and by 1946, all of the prisoners were returned to Europe and the camp was closed.

The most interesting element of this story is that the Nazis infiltrated the camp. They had lists of the POWs held there and managed to intimidate them by threatening their families at home in Germany. They used the POW mail office (also at Camp Hearne) to initiate secret communication with other prison camps. Driving through now so regularly, it's chilling to think that Hearne, Texas, had Nazis in its midst where now there's just a gas station, an antique place and Johnny Reb's Dixie Café.

Just nine miles after Hearne comes Calvert, which is about halfway between Houston and Fort Worth timewise. I love passing through Calvert, which calls itself a "quaint Victorian village offering a quiet, pleasant, relaxing glance back into time." It's obvious that the little shops along 6 depend on the fact that, for many of us, it's a welcome alternative to I-45 for heading north from Houston. From Boll Weevil Antiques to Common Scents candle shop, they've got cute names and catchy signs to flirt a little with the majority of motorists, who aren't locals. In an article that appeared in *Texas Monthly*, Paul Burka mentions the paradox that has arisen from this very thing. He notes that, even though shop owners oppose any detours off Highway 6 that would reduce tourist traffic past their businesses, the historic brick buildings are literally "degenerating, shaken by heavy truck traffic." So, as Burka puts it, the businesses can survive or the buildings can. I guess to have both would be like having cake and eating it, too. But what good is doing one without the other?

This day, with the rains a distant memory, the July sun exhibited a hot BMW Roadster—red, of course, and a convertible—parked on the street in front of an antiquated storefront with a really faded "Hazel's" stenciled on brick. Here was a juxtaposition of the exotic and brand spanking new with the withered and old. And such is the nature of the beast that both wants desperately for Highway 6 to keep its traffic and needs something else entirely. The very reason we go there is what's threatened most by our going there.

The original town had even more of a lustrous draw to it than what I see on my trips passing through today. The roadside historic marker describes a place with "swarming ox-carts and cotton wagons, busy stores and saloons, casino tables stacked with gold: this was early Calvert." I have a hunch that Texas towns will come full circle, eventually seeing casino tables stacked again with gold.

Calvert to Marlin is on a section of the Texas Brazos Trail route. The whole way to Waco, Highway 6 runs parallel to the Brazos River, which we can largely thank for the cities and towns that now exist along this drive. The river provided transportation (when it wasn't flooding), fertile ground for cotton and a source of life for the Indians. Today, it's a source of recreation in some spots, and it has been dammed up to make Possum Kingdom Lake, Lake Granbury and Lake Whitney.

This segment of our trip on Highway 6 cuts through Falls County, named for the Falls on the Brazos, where there is now a state park for camping, fishing and water recreation. A bloody massacre happened in this area on New Year's Day 1839, when members of the Morgan family, some of Marlin's earliest settlers, were attacked by Indians. This war party was composed of Caddos, Ionis, Anadarkos and Kichais and was lead by Chief Jose Maria on a mission to keep the whites out of the area they couldn't stand to lose; as it is still one of the most scenic parts of Texas, who could blame their resolve? All but one of the inhabitants inside Morgan's home were tomahawked and scalped. Stacy Ann Marlin, the one who survived, was wounded, and even though she pretended to be dead, the Indians did not take her scalp. The children had been outside in the yard, so they were able to hide and remain undetected by their parents' assailants. Isaac Marlin was the first of the children to reach the Marlin home, seven miles away from Morgan's Point, and it took him all night to do so. Two others arrived at daylight, and finally the severely wounded Stacy Ann arrived at noon. The Indians returned ten days later with a party of seventy warriors to attack the Marlin home, but they withdrew after seven of their own were killed by those inside whose lust for vengeance ensured their survival.

The result of the Morgan Massacre was what is now known as Captain Bryant's Fight (some call it Bryant's Defeat). Ranger Captain Benjamin Bryant was commissioned to lead a force of about forty-eight to respond to the chief's brutal raid. Just before it reached the Morgan homestead, Bryant's company encountered Jose Maria, who immediately fired on them, and a battle ensued. The chief took a bullet in the chest, reportedly right in his sternum, but stayed on his horse. One of Bryant's rangers shot the horse to bring Jose Maria down, but the brave warrior survived both of these attempts at his life. What happened next was mass confusion and a panicked retreat on the part of the rangers, who fled on horseback, leaving those on foot to be killed; there were eleven total. Reports indicate that the Indians suffered an equal loss. A few years later, the chief visited Bryant's Station to smoke a pipe with the captain, who allowed the chief to smoke first, acknowledging Jose Maria's victory in the fight that day. Jose Maria's tribes were constantly threatened by Wacos and Tawakonis, and he eventually entered into an arrangement with the Anglo settlers for protection from these tribes.

Up Highway 6, just south of Marlin, there's a roadside marker titled "Indian Battlefield" that describes Bryant's Defeat. Our path to Fort Worth from this point on (historically speaking, following Bryant's fight chronologically) traces the next encounter with Jose Maria's band: Colonel John Neill's Comanche Campaign. Equipped with forty days' worth of rations, the colonel led a large company of Texas Rangers on a campaign to pursue Comanche raiders, but they fought more than just the anticipated Comanches along the way. They crossed the Brazos and headed toward the Falls. From there, they went into the present-day Waco area, exactly the route Highway 6 takes motorists today. In late October 1839, Neill's troops came across Jose Maria's village right on the Brazos where Hill County is today. They attacked the village, and the Indians immediately fled. After taking their horses and supplies, Neill's company pursued the Indians along a route between the Brazos and Trinity Rivers, which would take them straight into present-day Fort Worth. Jose Maria survived to smoke the peace pipe with Bryant a few years later, but his group was scattered because of Neill's pursuit, and two of his warriors were killed.

Chief Jose Maria's band was stuck between a rock and a hard place: the whites were not their friends, yet other plains tribes were surely their enemies. But he was not alone in this conflict: the Wacos and the Cherokees had a fierce rivalry going on about ten years prior to the Morgan and Bryant fights. When the Cherokees arrived from Tennessee, camping along the northern Texas border, the Wacos ventured north on a stealing spree, raiding Cherokee camps along the Red River and retreating back to their villages in present-day Waco. In May 1829, the Cherokees paid the thieves back for their hostile welcome. Joseph Carroll McConnell provides a descriptive account of this fight in *The West Texas Frontier*:

Like demons who had dropped out of the dark clouds of night, the Cherokees stormed the village. Although greatly outnumbered, the invading enemy was much better armed, for they had only recently immigrated from Tennessee. The Wacos were soon forced to retreat to their own fortified sink holes, which afforded ample protection. The enemy held a council of war, and decided to storm these breastworks, fire their guns and then with tomahawks, fight the battle to a bloody finish. About this time, however, the Cherokees were charged by the thundering Tehuacanos coming from the breaks on the opposite side of the Brazos. The Tehuacanos captured a twelve year old boy, the only son of his father. This boy was brutally murdered, and his scalp placed on the end of a lance, which was used by the Tehuacanos to defy the Cherokees. The angered father of the boy stripped himself of all apparel and without a word, seized a knife in one hand and a tomahawk in the other, without heeding the protests of his companions, charged onward and said, "I shall die with my brave boy, by slaying the wild men who have plucked the last rose from my bosom." He rushed forward and before he fell successfully slayed a number of the Tehuacanos.

The harrowing scene that McConnell describes sounds like the final scene of a Greek tragedy, completed by a father's loyal yet tragic suicide. In this case, life imitates art, for Highway 6 was as bloody a path as any in early Texas, all the way through Waco and on up I-35 into Fort Worth.

The natives struggled. They struggled against neighboring tribes, vying for the rights to hunt certain grounds or camp by the rivers. They needed commodities, like tools, weapons and horses that these other tribes had, so they stole what they could find. They struggled against the Anglo-Texans, who wanted to build homes and churches, grow cotton and graze cattle and horses. Eventually, the whites wanted to build railroads. The Indians must have been astounded at the details and embellishments of these pale-skinned humans' lives. Even though the Indians didn't record their impressions in writing, I imagine they shared Thoreau's sentiments, for he thought the building of the railroad was silliness, reducing the humans, in their obsession with labor, to a colony of ants. In *Walden*, Thoreau said, "And every few years a new lot is laid down and run over; so that, if some have the pleasure of riding on a rail, others have the misfortune to be ridden upon."

Now, it's a rock-scissors-paper routine every time I get in the car and head to Houston. So rich with history, and far more beautiful scenery, 6 had always been my preference. But I've recently gone back down I-45 because, now that construction is relatively complete, it does save time. And at certain times of the year, you can grab a case of tree-ripened peaches in Fairfield right off the highway. I will always, however, recommend 6 to any driver who hasn't seen much of Texas. There are lush green pastures with livestock grazing, an invisible trail of blood underneath and, of course, all those little shops trying hard to stand erect so the trucks can't shake 'em down.

Early Settlements

In some ways the object of getting out of town is simply getting out of town and away from all the neon signs and billboards and fast-food places that accompany life in the big city, so the quickest and most direct is usually the best answer. For this trip, we took I-35 south to Highway 171 in Hillsboro. We set out to find an alternative to and from Houston, as I-45 can be intolerable, and what we found in the process is a storehouse of history that focuses mostly on the original Anglo migration into Texas, and the incredible challenges these people faced. They were from Kentucky or Tennessee; some were Czech or German; some were plantation owners; and all shared an unruly and stubborn resolve that facilitated their survival on land that several different tribes of Indians owned, at war with one another and at war with invaders.

Like the enticing sirens' song, which Ulysses only resisted by tying himself to the mast of his ship, Texas, it seems, was alluring and coveted by everyone who saw it, but not all survived this enchantment.

Highway 171 winds through the towns of Bynum, Hubbard and Coolidge. This part of the drive follows a narrow, curving path through mostly residential areas, with very little room for a view of the prairies beyond them, and if a photograph or sketch could render it in its entirety, it would look like a patchwork quilt. Each little lot of land is so different from the next: piles of rusting scrap metal, primary-colored plastic children's toys, a slobbering pit bull defiant at the end of his chain and an assortment of once-operating mechanical devices from fishing boats to lawn mowers to the cab of a pickup. In the midst of all this variance stands the pink or yellow or blue freshly painted two-story house with a porch swing and perfectly manicured lawn—its posture and mere existence smirking with derision at the adjacent patches on the quilt.

We drifted through Tehuacana, Texas, six miles northeast of Mexia. The town was named for the Tawakoni Indians, who inhabited this area until the 1840s, when white settlers began to stake their claims. This region once witnessed the brutal scalping of nearly fifty Tawakoni heads in 1830 when Cherokees attacked, led by Chief John Smith. The previous year, the Tawakonis caught several Cherokees trying to steal their horses, and they scalped them and tied their bodies to posts, performing a war dance around them. This bloody fight near Mexia was the result of Cherokee outrage and a desire for revenge. During the battle, the Cherokees had to fall back and hold a council— their difficulties penetrating the fortress that concealed the Tawakonis were beginning to sting of defeat. In *Indian Depredations in Texas*, J.W. Wilbarger describes the Cherokees' strategic siege:

The old warrior who advised holding the consultation made the following proposition: That a party of them should go a short distance off and cut some dry grass; that they load themselves with this grass, which would be a good shield, and then approach each hole in the fortress from the sides, and stop up the port holes with this grass. This they would set on fire, and they would in this way roast the inmates alive. The plan was agreed on and carried out. The smoke and flame rolled into the fortress in such quantities as to produce complete strangulation, and the inmates were forced to unroof the fortress and leap out amid the blinding columns of smoke. The Cherokees were stationed around, and slew them as they leaped out. The Cherokees would rush on the frightened and smothered Tehuacanas, and with their tomahawks and scalping knives they dealt death on every hand. A great number of warriors, women and children were suffocated to death on the inside. Many of the women and children were made prisoners, and but few of the men escaped. All the horses, buffalo skins, camp equipage, etc. fell into the hands of the Cherokees, who returned to their camp, making a wonderful display of their booty.

With a humble population of about three hundred today, Tehuacana's land has not been so paved and trodden as to completely cover the fiery remnants of its history. And the Tawakoni tribe was one of many who moved out of Texas to the Wichita Reservation in Oklahoma, sadly leaving behind only its name and the ghosts of the past.

We continued to wind through Limestone County, from Highway 171 to 14 to 39, until we came upon Molina's Restaurant and Tortilleria in Mexia, Texas. If you're anywhere near the vicinity, even 9:00 a.m. is a good time to stop for a taco. This place is worth the trip. A modest building with folding tables, chairs and linoleum floors, Molina's has an elaborate menu, stenciled onto a giant rectangular piece of metal and nailed to the wall. There is a seemingly endless list of breakfast plates and tacos and authentic Mexican *especialidads* for lunch. Several workers stopped in

Molina's.

to fill their stomachs and their ice chests, church families stopped by to pick up some homemade tortillas for lunch and a few locals came inside to exchange stories with the other patrons or to eat. There are shelves of candy for sale and a pretty big selection of beverages in several reach-in coolers, both American and Mexican favorites. The waitress was friendly, and we left there feeling like we'd unveiled a scandalous secret. We took a picture of the sign in front of this humble place, and even now, a glance at the picture or the mere mention of those tacos causes a smile to creep involuntarily across our faces. These are the things I've missed by taking I-45 down to Houston.

One of the prominent figures in the history of this area is a man who wore many hats. Atlanta lawyer Lochlin Johnson Farrar moved to Limestone County in 1859 to practice law in Springfield. By 1861, he was living in a hotel, with no land to his name, and his personal property was worth a mere $300. He formed the Limestone County Volunteers, a company that joined forces with the Twelfth Texas Cavalry for service in the Civil War. Farrar then served the Confederacy in the Red River Campaign when the Union attempted to seize access to Texas, and all of its exported cotton, via the Red River in Louisiana. Farrar worked in later years as a schoolteacher, a state senator, a judge and a member of the House of Representatives. It's striking how in the days of the Texas pioneers one man could rise and answer the call to leadership, like the point in the arrow-shaped formation of a flock of geese in flight. Forward the settlers flew, unified by their persistence and their desire to prosper; facing turbulence in many forms, their ranks were significantly thinned by the Civil War and by their fights with Indians.

Sixteen miles out of Mexia, at the junction for Highway 164 west, lies the marker for Personville. The roadside monument gives a few names and dates, but it could just as easily be summarized as follows: Here lies a tiny town whose population began with thirty people, rose to three hundred at its most prosperous time and was recorded as twenty within the last ten years, at which time they had one church, one school and one cemetery. Personville, it seems, has maintained the anonymity and solitude that its name suggests. Highway 164 will take you to Parker's Fort (also called, interchangeably, Fort Parker) in Groesbeck, but we continued south on 39 to North Zulch.

Our route down Highway 39 crosses the Old San Antonio Road, which at one time connected two Spanish missions between Nacogdoches and San Antonio. We passed through the tiny town of Flynn, where the roadside held three quick signs painted on poster board and faded from sunlight and rain: "Flynn Grocery and Feed," "Good Feed Ahead" and "Stop Here." Eventually we came upon a serene stretch of road just before Highway 90, where the Texas Brazos Trail and the Independence Trail intersect. The trees formed a canopy overhead. Cows lounged in the thick grass, legs folded underneath their stout bodies. Where just a few miles behind us sparsely populated towns cast their lots at the entrepreneur's game, here only nature revealed its existence, and it was idle and still.

We worked our way through Grimes County in the shape of a lightning bolt, taking Highway 39 to 90 through Singleton, Roans Prairie and, finally, Anderson. Two separate mail routes—one connecting Houston with Springfield and the other connecting Nacogdoches with San Felipe de Austin—formed an "X" where today's Anderson, Texas, now stands. Back in 1834, Henry Fanthorp built a two-room log house for himself and his wife, Rachel. They added more rooms to the building, and it became the Fanthorp Inn, drawing its customers from those who traveled the two stage lines in and out of Grimes County, and the inn also functioned as a post office when mail came through the area. The final vice-president of the Republic of Texas was Kenneth L. Anderson, who died at the Fanthorp Inn and for whom the town and center of Grimes County was ultimately named.

The Anderson area was also host to a Confederate gun factory during the Civil War. Originally from North Carolina, J.H. Dance and his two brothers moved to Brazoria County and started a company that manufactured a total of fewer than four hundred Colt-pattern revolvers, making the Dance pistol one of the rarest and most prized finds for antique gun collectors. The Dances sold their company to the Confederacy when they suffered from a lack of investors. The factory was then established just a few miles north of Anderson, and the last shipment of twenty-five Dance revolvers arrived in Houston in April 1865. After this final batch of six-shooters was manufactured and delivered, the Dance brothers quit the gun business and built gristmills and cotton gins. A photograph of Geronimo, the most famous Apache tribesman, shows one of these cherished Dance revolvers at his side.

The center of Grimes County saw prosperous growth, and businesses succeeded, but this rosy hue of optimism did not shield this area from Indian attacks. No one, it seems, was completely immune, and for some who lost their lives, it was merely a matter of being in the wrong place at the wrong time. Such was the fate of John Taylor, who lived in the area that is now Anderson. In 1836, he crossed paths with a raiding band of Indians, who chased and killed him and then mutilated his body. Delusional with grief and against the better judgment of all her neighbors and kin, his wife visited the spot where her husband was murdered, and she, too, lost her life to the Indians.

Passing through the tragic site, we drove down Farm Road 1774 through Plantersville, and into Magnolia, just inside Montgomery County. The town was first called Mink Prairie and then Mink in 1850. Next, the town was named Melton after a prominent landowner, but the postal workers were confusing it with Milton, Texas. Finally, an abundance of magnolia trees in the area inspired the townspeople to agree on the name Magnolia. Like many regions in the early settlements of Texas, Montgomery County's history is characterized by the kind of rises and falls of epic proportions that provide the plots for movies and novels. The French were here in the 1600s, and they recorded the presence of various tribes of Atakapan Indians. These tribes believed, poetically, that the first humans arose inside an oyster shell out of the ocean. These metaphorical "pearls," then, must have had a great reverence for how valuable and rare life is. It seems a contradiction to me, then, that the name of this tribe is a Choctaw word that means "man eaters." They believed that a man who was eaten by another man would have no afterlife, so perhaps they only practiced cannibalism to exact ultimate punishment on their enemies—to steal their lives and their hope for any further life. The Atakapan tribes blended with other tribes through intermarriage, and many died of the diseases that accompanied the European explorers; thus they soon faded out of existence.

Whites from Kentucky and Tennessee came next into Montgomery County, transforming the land from the free range of a hunting and gathering tribe of cannibals to the new, rigid hierarchy of the plantation. Landowners prospered on profusions of cotton grown by slaves, and two of the wealthiest slave owners in Texas lived here, owning more than one hundred slaves each. Naturally, things changed when the slaves were freed and labor had to be bought. The cotton industry died out, and the railroad came through. Several major railroads crossed through the county, and they enabled the success of the lumber industry. Before the clearing began, 80 percent of the county was covered with pine forests; needless to say, the railroad brought incomparable prosperity. And so the story goes, the ups and downs continued for Montgomery County as the Great Depression brought suffering and the oil boom, salvation. The county remains prosperous today because it brings in residents from the overflow of the Houston area's suburbs.

We drove into Houston to stop for the night. I learned early in life that there is no roller coaster so thrilling, no shark tank so threatening, no free-falling sky dive out of a plane so death-defying as driving on the major highways in Houston, Texas. My advice to those embarking on their inaugural trek: take the peripheral roads that form circuitous loops around the city's gravitational center and always have a plan for how you might go about abandoning your course on a few seconds' notice.

The next day—like a giant conveyor belt at an airport terminal delivering luggage, skis, golf clubs and crates of all shapes—the mighty Interstate 10 shuffled Fort DeVille, with us packed safely inside, westward through Katy and out of the great metropolis. We turned off at Highway 949 northeast to Farm Road 1094, and we entered arguably the most historically concentrated region in Texas, Austin County. It all began with the tenacity and vision of a father and his son.

Moses Austin obtained permission from the Mexican government to bring three hundred families into Texas and form a colony. He died of pneumonia before his dream could come to fruition, and in 1823 his son, Stephen Fuller Austin, took hold of the reins. Advertising in newspapers and spreading the word throughout the eastern states, Stephen F. Austin recruited wide-eyed and optimistic Anglo-American, German and Czech families to join him in Texas. I wonder what rhetoric could convince these men and women to embark on a harsh journey through inclement weather into a land unknown, occupied and ruled by a proud and dominant Mexico and inhabited by Indians, who for thousands of years sustained their lives by piercing intruders' bodies with arrowheads and who claimed trophies by slicing the scalps from their heads. Whatever his ads said worked, for they *did* embark, and Stephen F. Austin receives credit for the original Anglo settlement of Texas.

The Stephen F. Austin statue.

Once the frontiersmen settled in, so to speak, they began to hold meetings and organize themselves as a separate political body. They first expressed their displeasure with being ruled by Mexico in 1832 at San Felipe. In a remarkable illustration of the restlessness of the human spirit, never quite content with the status quo, they not only traveled to Texas from places as far as New York, but they also stood awhile—scanning the land and envisioning their houses and general stores and eventually stagecoach stations positioned strategically along creeks and paths forged by buffalo herds or even the Indians themselves—and they desired even more. They wanted a government made up of their own kind and no doubt fashioned after the one evolving in the rest of the states, so they formed two distinct entities: one to combat the Mexicans and the other, the Indians. The Republic of Texas and the Committee of Safety arose, which soon became the agency we know today as the Texas Rangers.

The capital of the republic was originally at San Felipe, and we drove within two miles of it on our way into Austin County. The townspeople burned their beloved town to the ground to prevent it from falling under Mexican control in 1836, and what resulted was a fast but furious war to be remembered.

In the great dense thickets of Texas history, the year 1836 proved to be contentious and bloody, to say the least. Not only did that year mark the beginning of the Texas Ranger and Indian wars, but it was also the year of the Texas War of Independence from Mexico. When General Santa Anna brought his army in from Mexico, general panic set in. News of the fall of the Alamo and the massacre at Goliad quickly spread. The majority of white settlers fled to the East in a mass exodus that was eventually named the Runaway Scrape. Sam Houston ordered what was left of his army to retreat as well.

Each family who stayed behind in a stubborn show of resolve was like one lone duck in the middle of a pond, ostentatiously vulnerable to Indian attacks while the military headed down to fight the Mexican army at San Jacinto. One family of German settlers who refused to run suffered a fate similar to that of the Parker family. In the midst of all the chaos, and exploiting the fear that Santa Anna's attempted conquest was creating, a raiding band of Karankawa Indians appeared at the homestead of Conrad and Mary Theresa Juergens. The Indians wounded Conrad and abducted a pregnant Mary Theresa and two of her stepsons. While a captive, she gave birth to Jane Margaret. Mother and infant survived their few months of captivity and were eventually ransomed. Conrad died within two years of the attack. Unlike that of Cynthia Ann (whose plight is described in the Parker's Fort drive), Mary Theresa's experience was short-lived, and she was not with the Indians long enough to become acclimated to their way of life. The monument recounting the Juergens family's experience is in present-day New Ulm, "the small town with a big heart."

At its conception, New Ulm was a German settlement, named for Ulm, Germany, by Austin's original settlers. We stopped at New Ulm's Texas Star Café for breakfast. A parking lot full of cars and trucks is always a good indication that the food will be all right. It seemed this was the place to eat in town, and everyone inside knew one another's names.

From New Ulm, we turned slightly south and headed down Farm Road 1291 to Fayetteville, which was a stage station on the Old San Felipe Trail at its inception. James J. Ross first established the station and subsequently the town, and his is a story of Austin's original three hundred that is as colorful as any you'll find. To begin, Ross liked women, and it seems that this affinity was the cause of most of his trouble. He married Mariah Cummins in Arkansas in June 1821, and she might have believed she was his first wife. A year later, he went to trial on charges of bigamy and proceeded with a divorce from a woman named Sinthia. He arrived in Texas the following year and quickly gained esteem as a landowner, a farmer and a captain in Austin's militia. He was a leader in the protection of the frontier, and he presided over several attacks on the Tawakoni and Waco tribes.

Just five years after Ross's arrival in Texas, a new scandal developed. He and his wife's younger sister, Nancy, were expecting a child. His marriage to Mariah fell apart, and he married her sister in 1828, just after he bought a league and a half of land in Fayette County. He built his home there, had four more children and founded the town of Fayetteville. But the scandal doesn't end there. Ross's notoriety mounted when settlers learned that he provided shelter for some Tonkawa Indians on his land. The shootout that resulted from this discovery cost him his life. What he left behind is clear: a legacy of a true frontiersman, the type who cannot be subdued by social constraints but will boldly make his contribution to what he perceives as the aggregate good. While his story might be slightly humorous, it is inarguably heroic.

Another of Austin's original immigrants alone confronted a band of marauding Indians and lived to tell the story. The account seems hard to believe, but perhaps the Indians were so stunned by his unmitigated rage and temerity that they let him live. As the story goes, Jesse Burnam lived right along the Colorado River and raised horses on the prairie. In broad daylight, one of Burnam's children witnessed the theft of all his horses and ran into the house to report the news. Jesse was bedridden with fever, but according to the story, he was so outraged at the Indians' audacity that he grabbed his gun, saddled his horse and headed out to find them. The enraged Burnam charged into the pack, shouting wildly as he fired his shotgun. If we can call it a strategy, it worked; the horses took off toward their familiar grazing land and Burnam let 'em have it with both barrels, as the saying goes. The Indians abandoned their chase, and he returned home without a single horse lost. We could say that he was mad with fever, but his story nevertheless creates a great tangible manifestation of the tenacious frontier spirit, the same spirit that read Stephen F. Austin's ad in the paper and said, "What the heck, we'll give this wild unsettled land a try" in the first place.

We drove through Fayetteville's town square, and I noticed mostly bed-and-breakfast signs and antique stores. This area prides itself in having the best antique shopping in Texas, sitting right in the middle of the "golden triangle" that connects Houston, Austin and San Antonio. They have a beautiful and well-preserved town square, and a sign entices visitors to "buy granite pieces of Fayetteville history."

We turned northeast onto 237 toward Round Top, passing the Sterling McCall Car Museum just before we entered the town. McCall started collecting old cars in 1979 when a 1927 Ford Model T Doctors Coupe rolled into his dealership, offered as a trade for a brand-new Corolla. He took the Model T, a 1941 Buick and a 1948 Lincoln Continental (both convertibles) to his farm, where he built garages in which to store them. His collection of classics grew enough to warrant the opening of a museum, and thus the Sterling McCall Museum was born, located just a few miles outside of Round Top.

On the front page of the community's website, a photograph of the road sign reads "Round Top pop. 77" and, printed over it in bold letters, "Who would have thought a town of 77 could offer the world so much to do?" As we drove through town, spotting well-decorated bed-and-breakfasts and antique shops, large artfully painted signs announcing the historical museum and the chamber of commerce building, which is a tiny one-room structure with a desk and a phone and a rack filled with pamphlets about area attractions, it became quite obvious to me that the main focus here in Round Top, Texas, is tourism. All seventy-seven members of the populace participate in some way in hospitality or the promotion of Round Top's history, which is of course connected with Austin's original three hundred. The town was composed at first of white plantation owners, dating back to 1826, and in the next ten to fifteen years, German settlers followed. The area was situated along a stagecoach route, and "the house with the round top" became a mileage marker along the way. Thus, the town came to be called Round Top.

Two structures in Round Top remind its seventy-seven residents of the town's origin: the Konrad Joh Log Cabin and the Old "Sam Lewis Stopping Place," which is now a University of Texas Research Center.

The Joh family's log cabin was built in 1848 of live oak logs, mud, sand and straw. In 1875, Konrad Joh used oxen to move the cabin uphill three hundred feet, where it stands today. Sam Lewis and his family occupied a cabin of cedar, which began as a two-room house and was enlarged to accommodate travelers from the stagecoach that passed through town. Lewis, his wife and his eight children welcomed frontier men and women who needed a meal and a place to sleep while their horses rested overnight. A roadside marker in Round Top's town square marks the memory of such frontier inns as this one, where strangers were welcome to share a family's meal and mail could be received and circulated in the area. Now, 150 years later, Round Top's residents proudly emulate the hospitality of the settlers, their artfully decorated signs drawing drivers in, offering the world so much to do.

As we left town, we merged from Highway 290 onto 390, where we entered Burton, a modest town in Washington County. We sidled around Lake Somerville and traced a segment of Yegua Creek, a Spanish name that means mare, where the rural scenery is postcard-worthy. We were not able to resist a visit to Dime Box, Texas, while we were in the neighborhood. In his book *Blue Highways*, William Least Heat-Moon describes his drive through Dime Box in the 1970s, having selected it for its curious name. He eats a meal of ham and beans and gets a haircut for $1.50 in what he describes as a "three-street town."

A woman at the post office explains the source of the town's name to Heat-Moon. The townspeople would drop a letter and ten cents into the box for outgoing mail. Thus, the town came to be named for its primitive postal system.

It's truly a quiet town today, with a population of about four hundred. Actually, this unpretentious place enjoyed a quick promenade in the national limelight in 1945 when 100 percent of its citizens sent dimes to President Franklin Roosevelt for the March of Dimes campaign. Aptly suited to its calling, Dime Box, Texas, was the first to fulfill the president's request. We drove through in just a few moments, and as we did, I wondered how the town has changed since Heat-Moon sat at a lunch counter drinking an RC Cola and eating ham in a four-calendar café while the patrons debated on the best method for killing "far ants."

Highway 141 ends at 21, where Old Dime Box once rested, the town's original location before railroad tracks arrived. This segment of

Highway 21 traces the King's Highway (El Camino Real), also called the Old San Antonio Road. Buffalo herds and Indian hunters originally forged the path that spanned one thousand miles from Mexico City to Natchitoches, Louisiana. In this region, where the Old San Antonio Road crosses the Brazos River, Highway 21 draws the line that created the northern boundary for Stephen F. Austin's colony, separating it from Sterling Robertson's colony to the north.

A little farther northeast on 21 lies the roadside marker for an arm of the Chisholm Trail, used for cattle drives from Texas to Kansas. This particular arm of the trail spans from Matagorda County, along the Gulf coast, to McGregor, just southwest of Waco. The Chisholm Trail was invaluable to the cattle industry until the 1870s, when the railroad reached this region.

We reached Caldwell, where the parking lot of Jake's Restaurant was filled to overflowing with cars and pickups. This town was named for a signer of the Texas Declaration of Independence, Mathew Caldwell. He was nicknamed "Old Paint" because he grew a speckled beard. Caldwell served as captain of a ranger company and fought Indians to reserve the early settlements for whites coming in from the eastern states. He fought in the famous Battle of Plum Creek, when the Comanches set out to avenge the wounds they suffered from the Council House Fight, in present-day Lockhart, which is located in the county that bears his name.

Just a few miles east of Caldwell on Highway 21 sits the site of Fort Tenoxtitlan, which was originally a Mexican fortress against white immigration. The name is an Aztec word that means "Prickly Pear Place," also the name given to Mexico City. The Mexicans believed that this location would be the capital of Texas, but they could not squelch the fiery spirits of the whites, who continued to populate the area in spite of Mexico's attempted line of defense. Mexican general Mier y Teran commanded the army at Tenoxtitlan, and when he became despondent over the realization that the whites would not be ruled, he committed suicide by falling on his sword. The Mexicans abandoned the fort in 1832, and whites subsequently used it as a fortress in Indian fights and as a trading post for the next few years.

After Prickly Pear Place, we drove northwestward on Highway 36 into Milam County, crossing through Milano along the way toward Little River. In 1839, the Texans won far too costly a victory over the

Comanches along this river in Milam County. Captain John Bird was in command of fifty rangers when he encountered twenty Comanche hunters. These original twenty soon multiplied into two hundred as Bird's company relentlessly, and unwisely, pursued them for many miles. An even graver error in judgment caused him to turn and retreat, giving the Comanches their opportunity to pursue and strike. Racing on horseback amidst a violent shower of arrows, Bird found shelter where he and his men could dismount and fire their rifles. The Comanches soon left the bloody Rangers to tend to the seven who were dying, one of whom was Captain Bird. The battle is now known as "Bird's Victory," although clearly the Comanches were the authors of this fate.

Our drive out of Burleson and into Milam County also crossed the thickets of Battleground Prairie, along the edge of Cedar Creek. In 1844, a mile-wide area of the prairie was awakened by the battle cries of Colonel Oldham's company of about thirty whites, as well as a group of about eight Indians. The Indians first encountered a few of Milam County's citizens, and both determined that their numbers were too few to chance a fight. The Indians turned back, and Colonel Oldham raised his company and went out in pursuit. They came upon the Indians while they were cooking terrapins over a fire. Dashing to their weapons, the Indians headed to the creek bottom while Oldham's men dispatched a couple of hounds to track them. The clever tribesmen buried themselves into a patch of soft sand so that their bodies would be shielded from bullets, and they successfully held off their opponents. Two of the white men, Mr. Reed and Mr. Bingham, did not survive this skirmish, and they are buried in Yellow Prairie, Burleson County. The prairies of the Cameron area are quiet today, though they still have that wild, unruly visage that signifies the memory of those sanguinary times.

From Cameron, we headed north on Highway 77 to 485 east to Farm Road 2027, painstakingly following the roads that trace the Brazos River. We drove past the Falls on the Brazos Park, and this is arguably the prettiest section of the river. While Stephen F. Austin's original settlers were busily claiming the land south of the Old San Antonio Road, Sterling Robertson's settled north of that line, and our road trip ran through these early settlements, all the way up to Falls County. In the winter of 1839, only two families and their extended relatives lived in this region along the Falls on the Brazos, the Morgans and the Marlins. The house of George

Morgan functioned as an unofficial fort where families surrounding his home could seek refuge during an Indian attack, and it is now named Morgan's Point. Several members of both families congregated there on the evening of New Year's Day when Indians entered the "fort" without a second's prior notice.

It would perhaps seem a simple decision to those of us who hear about their circumstances today, but those few survivors of the Morgan and Marlin families pondered whether to drop back to a more populated area in the lower settlements or fight the Indians and establish their ownership of Falls County once and for all. I can say with certainty which I would have done, and because we know that spirit that brought the first Anglo frontier men and women into Texas in the first place, we also know which they chose. Then it was the norm, but today we only see that kind of wild courage in the most reckless of gamblers or in the sword swallowers and lion tamers in circus acts. They had only their lives to lose, but they also knew the highest of stakes at which they would pay, since death could mean the stinging wounds of eleven arrowheads into one's chest and arms or the slicing off of one's tender scalp while he draws his last few torturous breaths. It could mean the capture of one's children and the theft of all his livestock and property. But like the truest and winningest of gamblers, the response inevitably was: "Look at what's to be won." These Texas prairies, intricately laced together with the creeks that stem from the Brazos, were a prize worth the egregious possibilities of murder.

The Falls County area served as a permanent area of residence for the Cherokees, who settled there in the 1830s. Then, Robertson's white settlers were also building homes on those prairies, so they lived relatively amicably alongside one another for a few years. The tribes who deplored the influx of whites to the region were those who, for hundreds of years, had used it as a prized hunting ground. Even today, the region's best asset is its land, and then it was invaluable to the tribes for its stock of wild game. The Marlins and the Morgans had their own blood out there on the table and rolled the dice; through an eventual treaty with Jose Maria's coalition, they won the lion's share. Our jagged drive along the Brazos sets a beautiful scene of the river's landscape in the foreground and the dramatic scenes from its history in the background.

After passing the Indian Battlefield, where a highway marker now sits as a reminder, we drove on Highway 6 through Waco and picked up 933 northwest toward Lake Whitney before reaching home. We passed the historic Fort Graham Cemetery, which was fortunately left intact when others were destroyed in the production of Lake Whitney. Fort Graham was built to protect the region from Indian attacks, but it served more as a hub of communications between other Texas forts. It also created a vantage point along the north–south line that connected the Towash Indian village (along the Brazos just north of Waco) to Fort Washita. Like many of the early frontier forts, Fort Graham's presence encouraged settlement in the area until it was abandoned in 1853.

Lake Whitney is a bustling area, probably because it is situated so close to the Dallas/Fort Worth metroplex. On a weekend drive, the roads are filled to their edges with cars and trucks towing boats in and out of the water. The map around Lake Whitney is dotted with camping areas on all sides of the snake-shaped water. It was very quickly clear that we were coming back into the neon and the urban sprawl that we had initially set out to escape, so we jumped on the interstate and raced the others back into Fort Worth.

The Texas Independence Trail

Try as we might, humans know very few things with absolute certainty. Most of us have realized that the only thing we can be completely certain about is that we will all one day die. Nietzsche said that "the certain prospect of death could sweeten every life with a precious and fragrant drop of levity." Presumably, our knowledge that nobody escapes death should make humans live with a certain zest unknown to other animals.

Even though it's a motivator for some and a bummer for others, I don't think anyone would dispute the certainty of our mortality. In most parts of the world, we can also be quite sure that the sun will rise and set with each new morning and night. Read enough about the gruesome obstacles the white frontier men and women faced when they tried to possess Texas exclusively—fighting not one but two powerful forces who also claimed ownership of it—and there's another thing we can claim with a pretty good proportion of certainty.

Call it certifiably insane or call it admirable—the fact remains that the white pioneers of what we call Texas today showed such a systematic and inexorable perseverance that, after hearing so many anecdotes that reveal the same seemingly unbeatable odds, we'd bet on their victory as surely as we'd bet that the sun will set this evening and rise again tomorrow. Give it as wide a point spread as you like; they just quite simply refused to give up.

A trip down to Houston gave me and Rick a reason to try a new route—the Texas Independence Trail. Reading about the places we passed on this trip, I've learned plenty about the whites' struggle, and their crazy courage under extreme duress makes me ashamed to have ever jumped at something as petty as finding a cockroach in the bathtub. Leaving Fort Worth on a gray January day, we followed our regular route to Molina's tacos before even planning our next move. There just doesn't seem to be a good reason to tamper with a working routine. This road trip varied from our other routes to Houston when we decided to follow the Independence Trail over to Washington on the Brazos State Park. But first we crossed to Navasota on Highway 105, where "horse breeding is as common as golfing."

Today's Navasota is fertile and green, quite a contrast to its beginnings, which were besmirched with heartache and disease. The crises began in 1865 when Confederate veterans set fire to a warehouse full of gunpowder and cotton. What resulted was an explosion that took out a good portion of the town's vitality, including its post office. Next came the wildfire spread of first cholera and then yellow fever, depleting the population of Navasota by about 50 percent. Further strife arrived with the Ku Klux Klan, requiring on at least one occasion a troop of federal soldiers to squelch this epidemic of hatred. Today, the town and its surrounding countryside enjoys a peaceful, if not prosperous, existence, the only mentionable threat being the endangerment of the Navasota Ladies' Tresses, an extremely rare stalk of tiny white orchids, which, as fate would have it, exist where coal strip mining now takes place.

We moseyed on down toward Washington on the Brazos State Park, where a sign instructed us to tune our radios to 91.9 FM for the park's information. Here we toured by car the state park that served as the canvas for Texas's original drafting and design. We passed the Star of the Republic Museum, a two-story building shaped like nothing other than a five-pointed star. On the day we visited, the museum library was closed, but it looks well worth a return trip during the week. Containing three thousand volumes, this extensive research library houses a rare and treasured collection documenting a thorough Texas history. Right outside the museum stands a statue of George C. Childress, the main author of Texas's Declaration of Independence and chairman of its delegation. It's a dramatic and mighty rendering of him, the fabric of his coat and thick waves of his hair ruffled as if by a turbulent wind. It might as well be a sculpture of Poseidon or Zeus, the powerful stern features bearing down upon mere mortals as they study its form.

We stopped the car briefly to take a couple of pictures of the horses grazing outside the Barrington Living History Farm. Barrington was the name of the plantation that Anson Jones, Texas's fourth and final president, occupied after the republic was annexed to the United States. Taking their cues from Jones's own journal entries, costumed interpreters have re-created life on Barrington Farm, complete with the authentic breeds of livestock from Texas's true lone star era. We did not witness this living history since we visited the park on a Saturday. It's a beautifully verdant and peaceful place, though, and I imagined for just a moment the layers upon layers of colorful cotton fabric on long-aproned women as they carry heavy buckets of water or baskets from hither to yon while the hems of their skirts lightly drag along dust-covered paths. I pictured the

The Barrington House.

Barrington horses.

proud Anson Jones, quill in hand, surveying the productivity of his peach trees, counting out two hundred bushels of corn and recording these notes in his journal. In these daybook pages, he wrote on one occasion that two slaves, Jerry and Mary, "broke up" cotton using an ox. I wonder if the interpreters who portray these slaves feel that hard, inexpressible tension that accompanied those whose long days demanded that they shoulder the heavy burdens of labor on this farm, with no time and no daylight left nor even the implements to record them into a journal. A pale-colored horse raised her head just midway as Rick's camera clicked. One soft, keen ear turned this way and that while we got back into the car and drove on through the park.

Washington on the Brazos was Sam Houston's headquarters for the volunteer army in 1835. By March 1836, the framers of the Texas Declaration of Independence arrived on the scene, desperate and determined to exercise their "right of self-preservation." When General Santa Anna took over Mexico, the Texans felt a very palpable threat to their autonomy as a republic, and they determined that, as unpleasant and costly as the task might be, they would rather fight for their independence than "submit to the most intolerable of all tyranny, the combined despotism of the sword and the priesthood." The names on the bottom of this document are those for whom counties and towns are named today, a permanent reminder and expression of deference for those who "fearlessly and confidently" declared our sovereignty from Santa Anna's military rule.

Caldwell, Crawford and Childress. I can imagine this convention of doctors, farmers, soldiers and pioneers as they earnestly brainstormed their list of grievances to be etched onto these pages. I can picture several sitting around a table, twisting their backs and crossing and uncrossing their legs as they attempted to craft the best phrasing that would express their contempt for the weakness of a country that would allow a brutal military to rule it. I can picture still others standing, one foot propped on a chair, elbow on knee, chin on hand, brows knitting and unknitting as they delineated the essential freedoms to which they believed we should all be entitled. And believe they did, beginning with this meeting of the minds at the state park where today actors relive the primitive ways of the farm life, and the best we can do to keep their memory is wander in and out of the angles of the star-shaped museum that records their names.

In 1843, President Sam Houston, honored leader of an independent Texas, dispatched an expedition to travel northward through the Texas plains and exhort all the native chiefs to attend a meeting at Bird's Fort, located in today's Dallas/Fort Worth metroplex along the Trinity River. Ever an advocate of peace with the tribes, Houston's goal was to negotiate a treaty that would be satisfactory to all parties involved. Colonel J.C. Eldridge, General Ham Bee and Thomas Torrey led the expedition, and three Delaware chiefs and a Waco accompanied them. These delegates departed from Washington on the Brazos in the spring of 1843 on what would become an exceedingly difficult journey. General Bee recorded their travels in a journal, an excerpt of which appears in J.W. Wilbarger's *Indian Depredations in Texas*. After many days of eating buffalo meat alone, with no salt or bread or rice, he poetically describes what provided their relief:

> *After wandering for many days over the vast prairies of Northwest Texas, in search of the head chief of the Comanche nation, but without*

success, we halted one morning in an immense plum patch to regale ourselves upon the delicious fruit with which the bushes were covered. Whilst busily engaged in this pleasant occupation, our attention was drawn to fresh plum skins on the ground, evidently quite recently pulled, and telling us that others besides ourselves were somewhere in the vicinity, who were as fond of plums as we were. This incident, like Crusoe's discovery of the foot prints in the sand by the sea shore, alarmed us a good deal and destroyed our appetite for plums, for we knew very well that any band of Indians we might encounter would be much more likely to prove enemies than friends.

Before we had come to any conclusion as to what was best to be done, an object approaching us was discovered. It proved to be a Comanche Indian, with a boy seven or eight years old, riding in front of him upon a magnificent horse. He came in right amongst us, and at first we were at a loss to understand why such a large, powerful man, as he evidently was, should be riding behind a little boy, but he informed us that he was totally blind, and that the little boy was his guide. He told us also of our near proximity to a large village of the Comanches (of which he was one of the chiefs), and to our great joy he told us it was also the village of Pa-ha-yu-co, the head chief of the Comanche Nation, the one we had been vainly looking for during the last three months. After the little boy (who was really quite handsome, dressed in his buck skin hunting shirt and leggings ornamented with beads) had gathered as many plums as he wanted, the blind chief started back to the village, accompanied by our Delaware Indian interpreters.

When I look at the Texas map, with its endless spider-webbed network of rivers and roads, it's difficult to imagine the land in its primeval state. After weaving through neighborhoods and past gas stations and country cafés for more than three hours, I can't even picture this peace delegation's route from Washington back toward Fort Worth the way we just drove, traveling days on horseback without ever encountering another human being, until the ground, speckled with the remains of half-eaten plums, gave the Indians away. However, unlike Robinson Crusoe, the white expedition did not so easily subdue the owner of those "footprints" to their will. Only in the most romantic of fiction would these dignified whites make willing servants of the savages.

Out of the state park, we took Farm Road 1155, curving in wide serpentine patterns along a pretty piece of Texas countryside. This road became for us another hidden treasure, a heads-up penny, as the horizon opened wider and wider to reveal a covert row of houses far off on a high hill beyond the trees. Hypnotized, I scanned the borders of the landscape while Rick guided the Cadillac this way and that, following the road. We passed a herd of cattle grazing, and just as we drove by, a herd dog lying by the fence yawned.

We made our way to Chappell Hill, Texas—"Welcome to God's Country." We passed Bevers Kitchen Café, with a painted sign bearing a buxom beaver wearing an apron and holding up a pie and a rolling pin, all the characteristic makings of some downright good cooking. After our drive, I read that Chappell Hill had a female founder, a rare occurrence, who named the town after her grandfather, Robert Wooding Chappell. Ms. Chappell's town played its part in the Civil War, as the Twenty-first Texas Lancers were raised here. Also, Camp Felder, a prison camp for Union soldiers, was located nearby. Today, the people of Chappell Hill are unified and proud of their annual events: the Bluebonnet Festival, Birdfest and, on the Fourth of July, "The Best Little Small Town Parade in Texas."

We passed up our opportunity for "country cookin" to follow a leg of the Texas Independence Trail south on 1371. We arrived at Bellville where, in the pines just north of town, a double hanging took place in 1896. The previous year, two murders happened in Austin County just thirty-eight days apart. Both of the accused were sentenced to death by hanging, so for the price of $22.30 the sheriff had a double scaffold built by one of his relatives. Both inmates were baptized and served a lavish meal of wine, chicken, ham, biscuits, cakes and pies. The townspeople bought tickets to attend this dual execution, though many more of the crowd just crashed through the cemetery gates, grossly outnumbering the paying patrons. Nobody, it seems, would miss the opportunity to witness the previously supposed-impossible feat of hanging two jailbirds with one scaffold. And according to legend, there was quite a heated deliberation about the destination of these two convicts, baptism or not.

Near those infamous pines, we drove through Bellville's town square, a quaintly inviting few blocks of retail shops, including the Four Roses antique shop and the Twin Sisters, a women's clothing boutique.

Originally I thought that the name surely signified that two sisters own the place, but there's another possible explanation. This region of Texas knows a famous pair of "Twin Sisters," a pair of cannons delivered to General Houston after Texas's painful defeats at the Alamo and Goliad. When those two gals rolled into town, I imagine Houston's troops were galvanized and ready to end this war once and for all. And end it they did, after just a month of training, at the Battle of San Jacinto on April 21.

Following the Texas Independence Trail from Bellville, we headed south on Highway 36 to Sealy, whose original prosperity was created by the sale of several leagues of land to the railroad companies. It was usually the case in Texas's early settlements that the towns that embraced the development of the railroads multiplied rapidly, while those that relied on the rivers eventually faded or had to relocate. Sealy thrived until a series of tragedies at the turn of the century stunted its growth. First, the Brazos River flood in 1899 brought severe damage. That summer, this region saw more than nine inches of rain in less than two weeks, and the river, whose profound embrace across the Texas plains was named the loving arms of God, couldn't hold that much water. The resulting flood cost 280 lives and the loss of countless homes. Next, the Gulf, Colorado and Santa Fe moved its headquarters out of Sealy and north to Bellville, taking a vital economy with it. In September 1900, the Great Storm, a Galveston hurricane, kicked 'em while they were already down. Economic recovery finally came in the form of the Sealy Mattress Company, still the major name in its industry.

Our visit to Sealy was quick, just a glance here and there as we crossed I-10 and continued south on Highway 36 toward Rosenberg. Another town that the auspices of the railroad created, Rosenberg developed when Richmond denied passage to the Gulf, Colorado and Santa Fe. The president of this railway, Henry Rosenberg, established the town at the crossroads of his railway with the Galveston, Harrisburg and San Antonio line. Rosenberg also was host to the headquarters of the "Macaroni Line," a railway toward Victoria built by Italian count Joseph Telfner—suddenly I can't clear my mind of the old song: "He stuck a feather in his hat…."

Passing quickly through Rosenberg, we turned east on 90 to Richmond, the seat of Fort Bend County. One of the oldest commercial buildings in Richmond is the old Sunset Saloon, which was built in the 1860s.

Another victim of the Great Storm in 1900, the Sunset's second story was ripped off when the hurricane's fatal winds sliced through town. Richmond saw its first railroad in 1855, when the Buffalo Bayou, Brazos and Colorado Railroad whistled and chugged its way through to Columbus. Things became a lot easier for travel and the shipping of goods when, in 1867, the people of Richmond built a railway bridge across a low part of the Brazos, making the previous and archaic use of ferries no longer necessary. Two years later, this very bridge became the gallows for a horse thief when vigilantes dragged him out of his jail cell one night while he slept.

While Richmond has a history that is all its own, and it once created a name for itself as a major hub in the cattle industry, today it blends with Houston. A drive through Richmond is rather indistinguishable from its giant, sprawling northeastern neighbor. But the one thing that does distinguish it in the grand scheme of Texas lore is that Richmond is the site of the grave for the woman who was named "The Mother of Texas" even before her death in 1880.

A young bride, Jane Wilkinson Long, married her husband, James, when she was just sixteen, and she left their home in Natchez to join him on the Bolivar Peninsula (near Galveston) at a fort built to attempt the liberation of Texas from Spain. The stories differ on the details concerning what earned her the title of the Lone Star's mother. Some accounts claim that she was quite literally the first English-speaking woman to enter motherhood on Texas soil, giving birth to her first daughter in 1821. Others attribute her nickname to her firm resolve when it came to standing side by side with her husband in his military endeavors. Determined to establish Texas's independence from the Spanish, she joined him at Fort Las Casas in Bolivar, and while he fought at La Bahia, she remained there with her children even when the others headed to the mainland when the fort's supplies ran dry. Upon hearing of his capture and death in Mexico City, she reportedly rode on horseback to appeal to one of the Mexican governors for justice for her husband's executioners.

An ever faithful widow to her husband's memory, Jane Long remained single, though reports claim that she was courted by Stephen Austin, Ben Milam and even Sam Houston. As a young bride, she waited for her husband's return patiently and stubbornly at the fort in Bolivar, and then Jane Long spent her later years in Fort Bend County until her death. She opened a boardinghouse in the Richmond area in 1837, serving as hostess for many of our history's VIPs, including a formal ball for Stephen F. Austin upon his return from capture in Mexico. She also ran a successful plantation outside of town, all the while refusing to accept a man's offer of marriage. A heroic and inspiring figure for her intrepid self-reliance, the Mother of Texas accompanied her husband in his quest to build this land as its own republic, even though his efforts were just slightly premature. She alone witnessed the transformation of Texas from Spanish rule to, finally, statehood. I looked at a portrait of Long in her later years, and through a plucky, eccentric grin, I could see the younger soldier inside, the one who gave birth alone to a child in a snow-covered, abandoned fort. I saw the one who kept her children warm and fed, literally living off the land by feeding them oysters and other seafood from the Gulf. Through that grin, I saw the soldier who cleverly tricked Karankawa Indians in the not-so-far-off distance into believing that the fort was occupied by men. I saw the aging widow who evolved into a shrewd and prosperous businesswoman, self-sufficient and determined to advance, leaving a legacy of courage and motherhood to the Richmond area.

From Richmond on Highway 90, we crossed the Brazos River and made our way into Houston for the night. The next morning, we followed I-10 west out of Houston, crossing the Colorado River at Columbus. We headed into La Grange and crossed a roadside trench where Tawakoni Indians once camped while on a horse-stealing spree. In 1826, Colorado district militia captain James Ross and about thirty men surprised the Tawakonis, who were in the midst of a war dance celebrating the acquisition of several bloody scalps. Ross's men killed eight and wounded a few others. An awkward twist of fate arose when, just nine years after Ross's bloody Indian fight, a mob of incensed neighbors murdered him for secretly harboring Indians on his land. There were few whose reverence for justice prevailed over their fear and hatred of the Indians.

Two years after Ross's militia fought the Tawakonis, John Henry Moore built two blockhouses in La Grange to serve as protection against future Indian attacks. Moore's Fort, as it came to be known, provided a refuge for area settlers when threats became imminent. Reproductions of Colonel Moore's blockhouses have been built near Round Top, just a few miles north of its original location.

Almost exactly midway between Houston and Austin, the landscape out here is hushed, docile. However, its climate can be as extreme as its scenery is beautiful. In a diary he kept as he traveled through Texas, Colonial Director of German Immigrants Alexander Bourgeois recorded his impressions of this section of the state, which he visited in July 1844:

> *We arrived in LaGrange on the Colorado at 10:30 a.m. Purchased provisions. The town is ideally located, at the center of the actual population of Texas. There are several businesses that carry a poor choice of merchandise at a very steep price. Terrible heat. Departed at 4 o'clock, crossed over the Colorado. The trail through the bottoms was difficult for our mules. The scenery changed. A splendid view, a magnificent valley at our feet ringed by neighboring hills.*

Splendid it was, and splendid it remains today; the terrain in Texas changes as if it had whims of its own. The only way to really see it is to keep a constant gaze out the window, because just as soon as you become comfortable with the inviting blankets created by flat, far-reaching prairies, fierce jagged mountains will burst through. There is a consciousness in this land that has been captured in the travel diaries of foreigners from all around, yet it still evades those of us who call it home. To me, the variety along these Texas roads is a subtle admonition that we are, after all, only human.

The landscape that decorates our drive provides only the set and backdrop for a far more colorful aspect appearing on the stage of Texas history—the players. Rick mentioned, as we drove through La Grange, that a famous brothel was once located here. It turns out that a savvy businesswoman from Waco, Miss Jessie Williams, bought a house on eleven acres outside the town limits of La Grange, and in doing so she ensured that it would be outside the bailiwick of both the local legislators and curious town clergy. Also, she was clever enough to stay on the more lucrative side of the law, as Will Lossein, La Grange's sheriff, paid a visit every evening to find out what criminals had been there to boast to the girls of their transgressions. The outlaws passing through sought redemption in Miss Williams's bedrooms as Catholics would at a confessional. And undoubtedly, with a police officer as dedicated to his job as Mr. Lossein, no crime went unsolved in Fayette County.

Miss Williams's brothel received its famous name, The Chicken Ranch, when the Depression era brought hard times with a shortage of cash. She continued to operate the house, charging "one chicken for one screw," until eventually her eleven acres were overrun with chickens; the girls ate heartily, and the customers, too, were satisfied. The story of The Chicken Ranch, reportedly the oldest continually operating brothel in the country, made its theatrical debut in *The Best Little Whorehouse in Texas*.

Out of La Grange, following the roads that run parallel to the path of the Colorado River, we took Highway 71 west to 21, where we picked up another segment of the Texas Independence Trail. At this very intersection, Bastrop County's first settlers built the river crossing at the Old San Antonio Road to Nacogdoches, which is now Highway 21. All the sources I've read confirm that Bastrop County was an area as hot as a habanero with regard to the volume of bloody confrontations with Indians. Because this region was the fall hunting ground for several tribes, the success of white settlement was significantly hindered, yet still they persisted. The land out here was just too pregnant with promise and too picturesque not to attempt to continue.

As early as 1830, such famous names as Josiah Wilbarger, Reuben Hornsby and James and Edward Burleson had settled in the county, and perhaps the most haunting of all Indian encounters is the story of La Grange's first settler, Josiah Wilbarger. After building a small log fortress to protect them from Indian attacks, he moved his wife and son, John, onto his league of land along the Colorado River. Until Reuben Hornsby arrived, the nearest family was seventy-five miles away, so far away that this spot on our route has a definition of independence all its own, considering that right now there are approximately five feet from the corner of my house to the corner of my neighbor's. Actually, when she waters her lawn on summer mornings, she can't avoid watering a strip of mine, too—which, incidentally, looks noticeably better-nourished than the rest.

Still living in a seventy-five-mile perimeter of solitude three years after he moved into the area, Wilbarger went out on a surveying expedition with a few other men. They were scouting out the land near Pecan Springs in preparation for the settlement of Stephen F. Austin's original colony. Indians spotted Wilbarger's scouts, and they swiftly attacked. He concealed himself behind a tree and fired his gun, but the tree did not provide adequate shelter to obstruct the arrow that pierced his calf and another that tore open his hip. As he attempted to run to his colleagues, who fled on horseback, a musket ball ripped its way into the back of his neck and exited on the side of his chin. I can't begin to imagine the excessive pain that Wilbarger endured, and what's even more shocking to me is that neither these injuries nor the more gruesome ones that followed were enough to rob him of his life. The account of Wilbarger's injuries and mysterious rescue appears in his brother's book, *Indian Depredations in Texas*:

> *He fell apparently dead, but though unable to move or speak, did not lose consciousness. He knew when the Indians came around him—when they stripped him naked and tore the scalp from his head. He says that though paralyzed and unable to move, he knew what was being done, and that when his scalp was torn from his skull it created no pain from which he could flinch, but sounded like distant thunder. The Indians cut the throats of Strother and Christian, but the character of Wilbarger's wound, no doubt, made them believe his neck was broken, and that he was surely dead. This saved his life.*
>
> *When Wilbarger recovered consciousness the evening was far advanced. He had lost much blood, and the blood was still slowly ebbing from his wounds. He was alone in the wilderness, desperately wounded, naked and still bleeding. Consumed by an intolerable thirst, he dragged himself to a pool of water and lay down in it for an hour, when he became so chilled and numb that with difficulty he crawled out to dry land. Being warmed by the sun and exhausted by loss of blood, he fell into a profound sleep. When awakened, the blood had ceased to flow from the wound in his neck, but he was again consumed with thirst and hunger.*
>
> *After going back to the pool and drinking, he crawled over the grass and devoured such snails as he could find, which appeased his hunger. The green flies had blown his wounds while he slept, and the maggots were at work, which pained and gave him fresh alarm. As night approached he determined to go as far as he could toward Reuben Hornsby's, about six miles distant. He had gone about six hundred yards when he sank to the ground exhausted, under a large post oak tree, and well nigh despairing of life. Those who have ever spent a summer in Austin know that in that*

climate the nights in summer are always cool, and before daybreak some covering is needed for comfort. Wilbarger, naked, wounded and feeble, suffered after midnight intensely from cold. No sound fell on his ear but the hooting of owls and the bark of the cayote wolf, while above him the bright silent stars seemed to mock his agony.

To explain how he survived and was eventually rescued, Wilbarger tells a strange ghost story. The day before the attack on his expedition, his sister, Margaret Clifton, had died in Missouri. She appeared to Wilbarger as he fought to stay alive, and he eventually realized that he was far too weak to travel to Hornsby's house. The specter of his sister told him to stay where he was, propped against an old oak, and that friends would rescue him before the next sunset. While Wilbarger was visited by this ghost, miles away Reuben Hornsby's wife awoke abruptly several times to exhort her husband to go out and look for Wilbarger. Her dreams were haunted with visions of him bloody and naked yet quite alive. At the insistence of his wife, Hornsby gathered a small party of men at dawn, and they rescued Wilbarger, who was partially alive or mostly dead, depending on the shade of the spectacles through which you see the world. Both horrifying and inspiringly mystical, Josiah Wilbarger's experience shows us what Texas's fight for independence from Mexico, and the white settlers' tug of war within these native-occupied, pretty mountains and plains was really like. They just quite simply refused to give up.

We veered a little farther off the beaten path when we cut south on Farm Road 535 in Cedar Creek, one of four towns in Texas to bear this name. The Independence Trail slides down to Rockne before turning back to the west. Named and renamed at least five times through its history, Rockne was christened in the 1930s when the town's students voted to use legendary Notre Dame football coach Knute Rockne's name, who died in the 1930s. Interestingly, in the 1940 film about Rockne, Ronald Reagan played George Gipp, one of the coach's star players, whose famous line, "Win one for the Gipper," became a political slogan in the '80s. The business of naming these tiny Texas towns may seem trivial, but an inquiry into the source usually leads down a tangent worth following, at least for a little while. Like a wayward end in a heap of yarn, a town's name like Venus, Maypearl, Dime Box or, for that matter, Old

Dime Box, will usually lead to a strange anecdote or caricature of the people who proudly live there.

The drive down FM 535 into Rockne is an Arcadian quest through unbridled fields, where rugged but docile longhorns stare drowsily at nothing in particular. These massive, muscular beasts in their constant pensive state have become a symbol of Texas. I studied them from the window of our passing car and wondered how their heads and shoulders can bear the heft of those mighty horns. There's something about these beeves that signifies the same dogged assiduity that made the Comanche tribes tighten their grips on the frontier while the white settlers struggled equally as hard to take it. Indeed, one major contributor in the eradication of the true Texas longhorn was the building of fences. They, like the natives of this land, thrived when they freely roamed the plains, but their numbers slowly decreased when fenced in and offered plowed fields that marked a human presence. Wholly unnoticed by the livestock, we passed them like the invisible breeze that bends the blades of grass and makes ripples in the water they drink, and still unnoticed, we cut back southwest on Highway 20 into Lockhart, the frequently professed Barbecue Capital of Texas.

Livestock around Lockhart.

Here, our road trip completed one part of the historical narrative we began on our homeward route from Corpus Christi (for the beginning of this narrative, see "Hill Country/Buffalo Hump's Raid"). After the raid of Linnville, down on the Gulf coast, and after Buffalo Hump's warriors surrounded Victoria, they headed north toward Lockhart. Like Icarus, who flew too high and melted his waxed and feathered wings, Buffalo Hump's unmitigated pride and the greed of his men led ultimately to their demise. Unwilling to leave any item of their loot behind—which included crates of ribbon and fabrics, iron for forging arrowheads and lawbooks whose pages only provided paper for rolling cigarettes—the warriors were at the mercy of the pace set by their pack mules, who were tired, slow and obstinate. A party of rangers met these uncharacteristically slow and heavily encumbered Comanches near Plum Creek. What arrived there to meet the rangers was a motley collection of Indians, looking both fiercely brave and absurdly weighed down by the ensemble that was their loot. In his book *Comanches: The Destruction of a People*, T.R. Fehrenbach paraphrases one poetic ranger's observations of the scene:

> [Jenkins remarked on the contrast between] *the grimly converging, silent lines of white horsemen,* [and] *the now-visible barbaric splendor of their savage enemy. The Comanche outriders wheeled and pranced, engaging in mounted acrobatics, shouting out their prowess and their mighty medicine, performing feats of horsemanship possible only to the people raised on horseback. Jenkins was caught up in admiration, and also struck by the grotesqueness of their appearance and actions. They trailed long red ribbons from their horses' tails; some carried opened umbrellas, contrasting weirdly and ridiculously with their fierce, horned headdresses.*

The commanding general, Felix Huston, described the appearance of the Comanches as "splendid" but relatively typical, it would seem. He records the scene with some admiration of the tribe: "I dismounted my men and a handsome fire was opened—the Indian chiefs cavorting around in splendid style, in front and flank, finely mounted, and dressed in all the splendor of Comanche warfare."

A Republic of Texas militiaman named Robert Hall, who recorded his memoirs under the pen name "Brazos," gave a more flowery description of the warriors in their stolen garb. From umbrellas to lace to coats on backward, the tribe sounds more like a group of children playing dress-up than an earnest war party of Indians:

> *The naked warriors had tried to dress themselves in the clothing they had stolen. Many of them put on cloth coats and buttoned them behind. Most of them had on stolen shoes and hats. They spread the calico over their horses, and tied hundreds of yards of ribbon in their horses' manes and to their tails. These Indians had been preparing for this raid for a long time. They all had new white shields, and many of the warriors had long tails to their headgear.*

Actually, one of the chiefs' caps had a fur "tail" that spanned an unbelievable thirty feet, according to the rangers who captured it.

The Battle of Plum Creek was a great victory for the white settlers, and as the militiamen returned home and the story spread from town to town, the details grew less and less clear. Some accounts say that the rangers defeated five hundred Indians, while others say there were four hundred, just as the five-pound bass becomes a fifteen-pounder when the moral of a story eclipses its details. One thing is clear: the rangers overwhelmed the warriors and routed them. When Huston's orderly lines approached, the Indians fled in all directions, trying to salvage what their pack mules humped alongside the band, and a chaos ensued that surely mirrored the silliness of their attire.

At Plum Creek that day, the whites had about two hundred men, including thirteen Tonkawa scouts. These friendly "Tonks" could be hired to help the rangers track and engage the Comanches, and they proved quite useful for this particular occasion when the Comanches grossly outnumbered the whites but were loaded down and distracted enough to be vulnerable. Brazos's "memoirs" include a rich description of the Tonkawas' means of celebrating the victory at Plum Creek. While he rested and nursed his wounds, the Tonkawas brought one fallen Comanche's body into the camp:

> *After awhile they began to sing and dance, and I thought that I detected the odor of burning flesh. I raised up and looked around, and, sure enough, our allies were cooking the Comanche warrior. They cut him*

into slices and broiled him on sticks. Curiously enough the eating of the flesh acted upon them as liquor does upon other men. After a few mouthfuls they began to act as if they were very drunk, and I don't think there was much pretense or sham about it. They danced, raved, howled and sang, and invited me to get up and eat a slice of Comanche. They said it would make me brave. I was very hungry, but not sufficiently so to become a cannibal. The Tonkaways were wild over the victory, and they did not cease their celebration until sunrise.

The natives' practices induced such consternation in the whites that their recorded observations of them, like what Brazos recalls here, often upstage the other, more mundane events in the frontier-era memoirs. The town of Lockhart saw this crucial battle fought and won in 1840, and free of Indian raids of this caliber, the town prospered heartily by virtue of its abundance of cattle (with beeves outnumbering people six to one in Texas by 1860). Not only were they abundant in Texas, the cattle were also quite cheap. Shortages in the North and East, where the meatpacking plants were situated, created a profitable demand for these beasts, overpopulated and tick-infested as they were. A longhorn worth two dollars in Texas sold for nearly twenty dollars up north. A major point on the Chisholm Trail, therefore, Lockhart produced several of its own herds to drive northward for sale in the booming Kansas market.

Skipping San Marcos, we veered northwestward on Highway 150 to cross I-35 on our way through Kyle, headquarters of the Texas Pie Company. Touting the motto "Life's short; eat more pie," Kyle's little neighborhood bakery has enticed people to place pie orders and hire catering all the way from Austin. Aside from every flavor of pie you could imagine, they package casseroles to go and serve home-style sandwiches for lunch each day. We could all use a reminder once in a while that life is short, so it requires a lot of sweetness. Who knows—this might be the very sort of levity Nietzsche was suggesting.

Texans who live in the Hill Country know all about such sweetness. Winding and climbing through Driftwood and on north to Dripping Springs, we experienced an ostensible change in the scenery. It'd be tough to argue this point with anyone who lives tucked away inside the tall east Texas pines or anyone who calls home the Big Bend's 800,000 acres of canyons and desert, but I think the Hill Country is the prettiest part of

Texas. Tiny creeks and full-throttle rapids alike grace the steep descents along the way, and there is no greater variety to be found. If you end up on the right stretch of a two-lane road, you're in for an amusement park ride, where some small surprise waits around every sharp turn or acute climb. By sheer accident, and certainly to our great fortune, we ended up on 3238 traversing the Hamilton Pool Reserve, which lets out at 962 westbound toward Cypress Mill. Just adjacent to Pedernales Falls, the reserve has such narrow roads that we weren't sure the Cadillac could stay inside the lines. What we stumbled onto was, I read later, a naturally formed pool created by a grotto that collapsed long ago from ages of water erosion. It was cool and shady, with sharp planes of sunlight cutting through at oblique angles as if an invisible hand, somewhere beyond those rocks and trees, tilted a giant mirror slowly this way and that. As we forged our way through this seemingly secret place, we both thought simultaneously, "How'd we end up here?" and, at the same time, "Who cares?" We found it, and we toured it, and that narrow little road was the most worthwhile detour we've ever accidentally encountered.

Highway 962 led us westward into Cypress Mill. Just before our junction with Highway 281, which would bring us north into the metroplex, we passed the location where a husband and wife, the Phelpses, were murdered in 1868 when a band of raiding Indians passed by Cypress Creek. Tom Phelps and his wife were fishing at the creek, but they did not heed the warnings of a young boy who came to report the sighting of warriors. Close by, and a few years earlier, two men were confronted by warriors while hunting hogs. Imagine their surprise, amidst the whine and squeal of a caterwauling swine that had fallen victim to their hot pursuit, when the commotion paused and Mr. Jackson and Steward looked up to discover a quiet warrior on horseback, watching from a not-too-friendly distance. What could have, a few seconds prior, been a comical and chaotic scene quickly turned to freezing, paralyzing fear. Mark Steward was able to flee the scene and escape, but Mr. Jackson was not so lucky that day.

After the site of the Phelps incident, our first stop on 281 was Marble Falls, where we immediately began looking for a place to eat. We have always been very lucky with the diners and kitchens we've literally stumbled upon, usually an hour after we started to think about food. But holding out for the place that seems just right has proven time and again to be the best strategy, and like our taco place, the River

City Grille in Marble Falls is one I've returned to twice since this day. Rick and I are willing to sacrifice good food for a good view, so when we saw the view this place offered, we didn't ask any questions except, "Can we get a seat outside?" The back patio of the restaurant literally hangs over Lake Marble Falls, a smaller segment of the much larger Lake LBJ. So, in shaded and breezy peace we dined on more than just passable food; it was good enough to bring me back. It's refreshing to know that an unfamiliar place can stand perfectly adjacent to a Chili's and be worthy competition for the Brinker megachain. I bet people sit all day on that patio like we did, watching the breeze press wrinkles into the sparkling water and watching ducks tread water and with clumsy nasal utterances boss one another around for no reason in particular.

What I did not know about Marble Falls at the time of this first visit is that its giant Granite Mountain, which is second in familiarity to the twenty-foot marble "falls" over the Colorado, contributed some of its pink stone to the construction of the Texas capitol building in Austin. This the citizens willingly did in exchange for a railroad route into Austin.

Highway 281 continues north into Burnet, site of old Fort Croghan. The fort was built after Texas's annexation to the United States, and it was occupied for a few years, though its dragoons saw no mentionable battles with Indians from the region. It was not built in vain, however, because the presence of the fort, as was the case with many of the frontier forts, gave white settlers a feeling of security that enabled them to move into the area and build their homes. The town of Burnet and, later, Burnet County developed well, while soldiers were stationed and ready should the need to protect their charges arise.

I camped once at Inks Lake Park, just minutes away from Burnet, and the rain had been so profuse that season that most of the campgrounds were completely underwater. The water was so high in some places that I actually saw benchless picnic tables as we drove through the park looking for a site. We pitched our tents on a base of wet leaves, labored intensely for a smoky, uncooperative fire and eventually gave up and went home. The river's floods would have surely been a blessing the majority of the time when Wilbarger and his friends needed a reliable water source, and it's these things, I've come to realize, that we now take for granted. Highway 281 runs alongside the Colorado and its reservoirs for most of the length of Burnet County, so the drive itself is really scenic when not cluttered with the traffic of families hauling boats in or out.

The next big town along our way was Lampasas, where the soil has seen bloodshed by whites who crossed paths with raiding Indian warriors and whites who battled one another, in the name of vigilante justice and drunken belligerence. What a time it must have been! On our road trips, Rick and I often eat silent breakfasts while we listen to the locals interact. There's absolutely no limit to the span of topics disputed and settled on a Saturday morning over bacon, eggs and cigarettes in a small town's hopping café. Even though I love to hear these conversations, I'd love even more to hear those that took place in these cafés in the middle of the 1800s when, among other things, the Horrell-Higgins Feud was underway. They ought to make a movie of this one, which includes a cattleman named Pink Higgins and a gunfight in the Gem Saloon.

Evidently, the four Horrell brothers—Tom, Mart, Merritt and Sam—were a delinquent bunch, accused on many occasions of murder and stealing cattle. Those days, these two crimes weighed about the same in the minds of most. Things got ugly when Ben, Tom and Mart interfered with a posse of lawmen who were trying to apprehend two men, the Short brothers, for shooting an officer. To calm things down, Lampasas officials asked for help from the state, and what resulted was a ban on carrying guns in town. In March 1873, to enforce the new sanction, Texas state police entered the Lampasas Saloon, where the Horrells were interrupted from their carousing. The gunfight that followed took the lives of four officers, and the Horrell gang was soon on the run. Somehow, the law got a hold of Mart Horrell and a few other men connected to the gunfight. By May, though, the other three raided the jail, released their brother and his accomplices and headed to New Mexico until things quieted down. A year later, they returned, and two years later, they were tried for their crimes but found not guilty.

I can just picture that scene in the Lampasas Saloon. The writers of the old spaghetti westerns couldn't dream of making this one up. I can see the Horrell gang at the bar, their backs to the room, Sam leaning on an elbow and Merritt, with one knee raised, propping one dusty boot up on the edge of the barstool he stands next to. Mart sits, eyes glassy, spinning a little as drunks do when they raise their heads to growl out a phrase. Tom mashes a cigarette out with his toe; then all four simultaneously toss back a copper shot of whiskey before turning around to see why the place got so silent all of a sudden. There stand the state police, tall and stern, arms akimbo, feet planted confidently and soberly. Words are exchanged and bullets fly.

The gang met their match a few years later when Pink Higgins accused them of stealing his cattle. Higgins got a posse of like-minded and law-abiding citizens to help him pursue the Horrells and bring them to justice. Angry and apparently unafraid, Higgins entered the Gem Saloon and shot Merritt Horrell, killing him. After an unknown party, clearly part of Higgins's gang, ambushed Tom and Mart while they headed into town one day, things heated up. Higgins never had to answer for the assault because, conveniently, somebody burglarized the Lampasas county clerk's office and destroyed all the records. After that, the feud came to a head when both sides, now significantly larger in numbers, battled it out on the town square. The battle cost a life on each side. Rangers arrived on the scene and forced a treaty between the remaining three Horrells and Pink Higgins. Tom and Mart were later murdered in a jail cell by vigilantes, so only Higgins and Sam Horrell got to see old age.

The Saturday morning gatherings over bacon and eggs would have sounded much more dramatic back then, and it wouldn't be because they're thinking about changing the route of the annual Christmas parade.

I love that drive up 281, and Lampasas is still Hill Country territory, so there's a lot of beautiful landscape to take in. The blood has long been washed away.

Our next major town, also a county seat, is Hamilton. There were a few conflicts in this town, but none of the caliber of those in Lampasas and none requiring national attention. A historical marker in town describes the way life was during Civil War times, and I'm sure these primitive accommodations existed in many of the area's towns. It's a great visual depiction, though, and it reinforces my surprise at the tenacity of those who built today's Texas. Without the comforts of electricity and mechanized farm equipment, it's hard to believe that they persisted, but like the rising and setting of the sun, persist they did. Part of the marker reads:

During the Civil War, travel was on horseback and hauling by ox wagon. Homes were of logs split from timber along creeks and rivers. About half an acre a day was farmed with homemade wooden tools.

Corn and wheat were raised. On burned-over ground each family grew its own tobacco, hanging the leaves inside the living room to dry. Diet was mostly beef, cornbread and coffee substitutes. Homes were lighted by wicks stuck into tallow-filled eggshells. With few men on hand to brand and herd, feuds rose over thefts and straying cattle.

The marker goes on to describe the displaced Confederate deserters who fled to Mexico for solace only to return later to garner support for their anti-Texan sentiments, clearly an unsuccessful endeavor. We didn't get the slogan "Don't Mess with Texas" only on account of a profusion of litterbugs.

The last major town before our homeward stretch on I-20 was Stephenville, which is just one hundred miles from Dallas. There were many near-death experiences among the people in and around Stephenville. One of these was the attack on the Wilkins family in 1867. The Indians chased and almost caught the Wilkins's son, who made it home in the knick of time. His mother came outside and, in an insane spell of courage, yelled out to the warriors who chased her son. It's quite a sight to imagine: Mrs. Wilkins, red-faced and arms flailing, angrily scolding these painted giants on horseback and commanding them not to shoot her dog. Completely unscathed by her matriarchal rants, one Indian aimed and shot an arrow right at her, hitting the fence post by which she stood. Two near misses in one day were enough to convince George Wilkins to sell his herd, pack up his family and head back to east Texas, where things were a little quieter.

About five years prior to the Wilkins's attack, a few of Stephenville's citizens succeeded in ambushing a band of horse thieves, also an insanely courageous undertaking. The whites shrewdly headed southeast and concealed themselves in a rock crevice called the Motheral Gap. Two or three of the even more daring volunteered to track the Indians and their loot—several stolen horses. The resulting battle was a victory for the whites, and they were even so bold—better yet, so full of lust for vengeance—that they scalped one of the warriors they wounded.

The only kind of wildness that we'd find today in Stephenville would occur at a frat party at Tarleton State. If only the rocks and fence posts could speak, they'd tell how, with mouths agape, they watched the whites defend their lives against a frightening and unfamiliar opponent.

However, as the stories continue to show, even far north of the Independence Trail, they just quite simply refused to give up. The certainty of death liberated them, and the sweetness often came at a heavy price.

Hill Country/Buffalo Hump's Raid

It was a Saturday morning with dark skies and rain in Fort Worth. Rick's policy is this: if you don't like the weather you've got, go south. So we took 377 through Granbury into Stephenville, and by the time we got to Dublin, Texas, the skies had cleared and the sun was lighting Dublin's newly rain-washed Dr. Pepper billboards. They're bright red, vintage-looking ads that have the same effect as the old Coppertone pictures of the puppy and the little girl. One showed a girl in a red dress on a swing, which moved back and forth across the billboard. A prosperous little town, Dublin has its claim to fame, boasting the only manufacturing plant of the "real" original Dr. Pepper made from pure cane sugar.

In Comanche, we picked up Highway 16, which crosses the South Leon River and cuts through the town of Priddy. As even its name suggests, Comanche, Texas, is a significant dot on the map of pioneer history. Today, "Old Cora" still stands, the oldest existing original courthouse in Texas, named after the first seat of Comanche County. Beside the courthouse sits the "Fleming Oak," guarded by the ten-gauge shotgun of pioneer Mart Fleming, who claimed that the tree saved his life when Indians attacked. Comanche also lies on the route of the Texas Forts Trail because pioneer Texans grazed their oxen through this region on their way along the Fort Phantom Hill road. B.W. Aston and Donathon Taylor describe the early days of Comanche, Texas, in their book *Along the Texas Forts Trail*:

The Dr. Pepper sign.

Comanche was then plagued with lawlessness—notably the killing of a deputy sheriff by the infamous outlaw John Wesley Hardin. Citizens formed a mob and hanged Joe Hardin, the gunman's brother, along with four of the gunman's friends. John Wesley escaped for the time and later got off with a sentence of twenty-five years in prison. Law and order were soon restored to the community.

As Highway 16 exits Priddy, the road drops down to forge its way through thick walls of rock. This section is a painter's muse—the variegated layers of rock, clay and dirt create a spectrum of swirling colors. When the margins open and the road rises out again, a bridge takes you across the San Saba River and into Llano County, the deer capital of Texas. Present-day offerings include the Badu House bed-and-breakfast and Monk Daddy's Grille right on the Llano River. But a drive through Llano County on Highway 16 also touches the place where, only three or four generations prior, the local citizens spread word of the Packsaddle Mountain Fight and the mystery of Babyhead Mountain. In August 1873, an arrow stuck in the side of a cow foretold the presence of Indians and the fight that would ensue. Eight cowboys fought twenty-one Apache Indians on Packsaddle Mountain, about fifteen miles east of the town of Llano.

The story of Babyhead Mountain wears a veil of mystery, as several different, but equally vague, stories have arisen from the locals and their descendants. While even the dates are unclear, ranging from 1850 to mid-1870s, the one detail of the story that remains consistent is this: the severed head of a baby girl was found impaled on a stake on what is now called Babyhead Mountain. Some stories blame the Indians; others blame white conspirators with various motives, and only the victim remains consistent, the namesake of both the mountain and a nearby cemetery, whose first burial was also that of a child.

The weather was still on our side as we cruised past the legendary "mountains," so we turned off at Highway 965 toward Fredericksburg via Enchanted Rock, a pink granite exposed rock formation rising 425 feet above its surroundings. Once a landmark touched by Indians, Texas pioneers and even Jack Hays, it is now an attraction for outdoor adventure seekers. There are campsites, a habitat for local wildlife and a four-mile hiking trail that goes to the top of the colorful "mountain." The official website gives a few historical anecdotes about how the rock came to be enchanted:

> *Tonkawa Indians believed ghost fires flickered at the top, and they heard weird creaking and groaning, which geologists now say resulted from the rock's heating by day and contracting in the cool night. A conquistador captured by the Tonkawa described how he escaped by losing himself in the rock area, giving rise to an Indian legend of a "pale man swallowed by a rock and reborn as one of their own." The Indians believed he wove enchantments on the area, but he explained that the rock wove the spells. "When I was swallowed by the rock, I joined the many spirits who enchant this place."*

The shape of Enchanted Rock enabled Jack Hays to survive an Indian attack while he was separated from his group on a surveying expedition. He ran to the top and, concealing himself in its huge crevice, single-handedly held at bay several Indians. They eventually retreated, as he was a skillful shot from that vantage point, killing several before they were ever in close enough range for him to use his famous revolver.

Enchanted Rock.

We took a fast look at Fredericksburg, but you could spend an entire weekend there. It would take a couple of days just to see all the shops and sample the selection of restaurants, ranging from popular chains to unique little family-owned German cafés. The more modern history buffs could spend all day at the World War II memorial museum honoring Admiral Nimitz. The *Texas State Park Guide* gives an informative description:

> *The Nimitz Hotel in the heart of Fredericksburg was the boyhood home of Chester W. Nimitz, the fleet admiral who led the Navy to victory in the Pacific during World War II and signed the Japanese surrender documents. The Nimitz family's steamboat hotel is the historic centerpiece of this site on Fredericksburg's Main Street. Now part of a nine-acre museum complex that showcases over 30,000 square feet of exhibits, the site is home to the world's foremost museum on the United States' involvement in the Pacific War. Visitors can saunter through the exhibits that include a captured Japanese midget sub, a life-sized army camp in the South Pacific, authentic Allied and Japanese artifacts or they can sit in a Japanese Garden of Peace.*

Nearly a century before the dawn of World War II, however, the settlers of Fredericksburg made peace with the Comanche Indians. A roadside marker commemorates the Easter Fires, which were originally lit by Comanches in the hills of Fredericksburg to signal their 1847 treaty with the whites. You can still see the fires today at Easter time on Cross Mountain, a giant limestone hill that was used as a Comanche smoke-signaling post and as a navigation point for the Spanish on their way from San Antonio to the San Saba mission. A nearby roadside marker elaborates:

> *This marl and limestone hill, elevation 1,915 feet, was an Indian signal point, advancing news of the intrusions of white settlers. The hill was first recorded and described by the German geologist, Dr. Ferdinand Roemer in 1847. A timber cross found on the hilltop the same year suggests that Spanish missionaries recognized it as a landmark on the path from San Antonio to Mission San Saba. John Christian Durst (1825–1898), arriving with his family in 1847 from Germany, received a town lot and 10 acres of land, including this hill. On finding the cross, he named it "Kreuzberg," or Cross Mountain. The Easter fires on Cross Mountain and the surrounding hills recall a German tradition of burning the old growth to make way for the new, and also commemorate the 1847 treaty made by John O. Meusebach and the settlers to establish peace with the Comanche nation. In 1849, a Bohemian priest, Father George Menzel, erected a more substantial cross as a symbol of redemption and civilization. Easter Sunrise Services were held on the mountain for many years prior to 1941. In 1946 the Very Rev. F.X. Wolf threw the switch to illuminate the permanent cross of metal and concrete built by St. Mary's Catholic Church.*

While the cross on Cross Mountain was their reference point along the way, the Pinta Trail conveyed the Spanish north to their mission in San Saba. Outside Fredericksburg on Highway 290, just east of town, sits the location of the old Pinta Trail and the site of Fort Martin Scott, both reminders of the time when the town was first established.

Fort Martin Scott saw several confrontations with Indians and operated to protect the inhabitants of Fredericksburg from Indian attacks. While the Comanche nation honored its treaty after 1847, the townspeople still feared the Kiowas, and the military brought troops in to man the fort in

1848. Unfortunately, the fort's presence did not prevent tragedy in 1864, when the McDonald Massacre took place. The Kiowas killed two and abducted others in this raid, which occurred in August in the town of Harper, west of Fredericksburg.

On Highway 16 heading southwest out of Fredericksburg, we crossed the Guadalupe River just as we entered the town of Kerrville, where you can "Lose your heart to the hills." Kerrville became known as the mohair capital of the world due to the thriving, prolific business of the Y.O. Ranch. The Y.O. Ranch Hotel and Convention Center was the first thing I noted as we drove into town.

Several stories of encounters with Indians have been passed down from the first inhabitants of the Kerrville area and surrounding Kerr County. In 1868, two women, Mrs. Wachter and Mrs. Alexander, were attacked by Indians while their husbands were away from home. Our drive on Highway 16 is surely similar to the route these men took, who headed northwest into Fredericksburg for business. Mrs. Wachter was shot in the shoulder, but she survived, while Mrs. Alexander was murdered and her body was burned. Ten years earlier, in 1858, about five miles west of Kerrville, Indians attacked Rolland Nichols while he was out hunting for turkeys. The year before, a group of seven Kerrville men pursued a band of raiding Indians along the Guadalupe River. While the men camped one night, the Indians caught them by surprise, took their weapons and attacked. One of the men was killed, and all but one were badly injured. Some suffered from their wounds for more than twenty years after the incident. These stories remind us that these lands witnessed a bloody past, not altogether distant, where today livestock freely roam and businesses prosper.

We continued on Highway 16, which, like a Colorado Rocky mountain pass, winds around sharp, narrow curves. Don't miss this section of the drive by taking the shortcut on 173! It's a mixture of high Bandera mountain walls and vast ranch lands. For the passenger gazing out the window, this depicts a thrilling contrast of impenetrable, treacherous rock and idyllic views of sleepy-eyed, grazing cows. The peace remains until the outskirts of San Antonio, and Highway 16 will take you straight into the center of the city. We dropped down on Loop 1604 and picked up 16 on the south end of town. Our drive through Bexar County gave us an opportunity to pass two sites related to the crucial events from the tale of how Texas as we know it came to be.

San Antonio was a critical location in the Texas War of Independence, hosting two of its four major battles. The first of these was the Storming of Bexar (the original name of San Antonio) in December 1835. The battle began on a December morning when 300 volunteer Texans attacked about 1,200 Mexican troops. After three days of fighting, the Texan troops took a priest's house in the Main Plaza, causing the Mexicans to retreat to the Alamo and send out a white flag. They signed a truce, but it didn't last long. The fall of the Alamo and the massacre at Goliad followed this victory, and eventually Texas won its independence at the Battle of San Jacinto just east of present-day Houston.

After the Texans seized Bexar, and General de Cos surrendered, they occupied the Alamo in the central part of San Antonio, used as a mission for the previous one hundred years. The following description of what happened next is from the Alamo's official website:

> On February 23, 1836, the arrival of General Antonio Lopez de Santa Anna's army outside San Antonio nearly caught them by surprise. Undaunted, the Texans and Tejanos prepared to defend the Alamo together. The defenders held out for 13 days against Santa Anna's army. William B. Travis, the commander of the Alamo sent forth couriers carrying pleas for help to communities in Texas. On the eighth day of the siege, a band of 32 volunteers from Gonzales arrived, bringing the number of defenders to nearly two hundred. Legend holds that with the possibility of additional help fading, Colonel Travis drew a line on the ground and asked any man willing to stay and fight to step over—all except one did. As the defenders saw it, the Alamo was the key to the defense of Texas, and they were ready to give their lives rather than surrender their position to General Santa Anna. Among the Alamo's garrison were Jim Bowie, renowned knife fighter, and David Crockett, famed frontiersman and former congressman from Tennessee.
>
> As the Texans were grossly outnumbered and sorely defeated, the Alamo is now a symbol of courage that surpasses any other in Texas history. It is the symbol of "a heroic struggle against overwhelming odds," and the men who died there, martyrs.

There is another, less famous, historical event that occurred in the center of San Antonio, and it carries with it the sting of rash actions and misunderstood intentions. The bloody, heated "Council House Fight" happened in a small limestone building right next to the San Antonio jail, which came to be known as the Council House after what happened there in 1840.

Colonel Albert Sidney Johnston requested a conference with the Southern Comanches in an attempt to recover dozens of Texas captives. Twelve principal chiefs came to San Antonio expecting such tribute as the Mexican and Spanish had always provided at these gatherings. They hoped to receive some Colt revolving pistols that provided Hays and his men "a shot for every finger" in their storming victories against their tribe. They were told that there would be an exchange of captives, so they brought two stolen children to start the negotiations. The revulsion the Texans felt when confronted with these mutilated, half-living creatures incited immediate and bloody revenge.

In *Comanches: The Destruction of a People*, T.R. Fehrenbach describes the scene at the onset of the negotiations. He illustrates a feeling of apprehension but also genuine cooperation on the part of both the Indians and the whites:

> *The twelve war chiefs, led by Mook-war-ruh, arrived in their finest attire, painted for a ceremonial occasion. They squatted on the dirt floor across from the delegation of Texan commissioners and local officials, exchanging greetings through an interpreter. Outside, in the courtyard, the Comanche women, also painted and dressed in their most colorful costumes, squatted patiently; the young boys began to play war games in the dusty street. A large crowd of curious spectators, Anglos and native San Antonio Mexicans, gathered to watch the proceedings. Men tossed coins in the air for the Comanche boys to use as marks for their miniature arrows. The mood of the onlookers was not hostile, but overwhelmingly curious—everyone wanted to see the strange and dreaded Indians.*

What soon developed was a shower of arrows and a haze of musket smoke after the whites tried to hold the chiefs hostage and use them as leverage for the return of all the Comanche captives. Even the women and children outside the Council House were fired upon and fighting back. Fehrenbach describes the final scene of this unfortunate and irreparable occurrence:

In the last stages, the fight became a hunt. Two warriors who barricaded themselves in a cookhouse were surrounded by angry whites. When they refused to come out, the little building was set afire with turpentine. As the two were forced out by the flames, one's head was split by an ax, the other shot. No Comanche escaped the soldiers and mob. Thirty-three chiefs, women, and children died in this massacre. Thirty-two, all women and children, many wounded, were seized and thrown into jail. Seven whites had been killed, including an army officer and the San Antonio sheriff. Ten others were badly wounded, and many whites, officials and onlookers, had suffered minor hurts. In the shocked aftermath of the bloodbath, the single surgeon in San Antonio, an immigrant German, worked through the night to save the injured whites.

While the whites believed that the Comanches should return all captives in exchange for a peace treaty, the Comanches thought that the return of two was a great concession and that they should receive gifts in exchange for the rest. On this fateful day in San Antonio, what began as an opportunity for both sides to profit ended in feelings of hatred and anger that nothing could ever repair. The Council House Fight incited the vengeance of Chief Buffalo Hump, whose angry raid spanned much of the same area we covered on this road trip.

From Loop 1604 around the western border of San Antonio, we took Interstate 37 down to Corpus Christi. I-37 crosses through Atascosa County, named for a Spanish term describing boggy ground that hinders travel. This route touches a point along El Camino Real, or the King's Highway. Also called the Old San Antonio Road, this route dates back to 1722, and it stretched nearly one thousand miles, spanning from the Mexican border to Louisiana. Another historic highway would have shadowed our drive to Corpus Christi: the Old Alice Road, running from San Antonio to Brownsville at the southernmost tip of Texas, where the Rio Grande meets the Gulf of Mexico. A busy, popular route, it was originally forged by Indian tribes and then used by Spanish expeditions, widened by Mexican oxcarts and, in the 1860s, became a stage route.

Corpus Christi was a perfect overnight stopping place for us, and you could spend another day there enjoying the Gulf beaches and visiting historic landmarks throughout Nueces County. First of all, this region along the coast of the Gulf of Mexico hosted its own indigenous Indian tribe, the

Karankawas, who inhabited the stretch of land from Galveston to Corpus Christi. The existence of these Indians was noted as early as 1528 when explorer Cabeza de Vaca shipwrecked in Texas. In downtown Corpus Christi, a roadside marker memorializing this tribe provides a good description:

> *A primitive tribe, the Karankawas fished and gathered roots and cactus fruit for food. The men were usually tall and wore their hair long or braided with colorful bits of flannel and rattlesnake rattles. The women were shorter and stouter. The Indians often smeared their bodies with alligator grease and dirt to repel mosquitoes. At first friendly to Europeans, they later gained a reputation for savagery. Persistent reports that the Karankawas were cannibals may be traced to occasional ritualistic practices.*
>
> *Attempts by Spanish Franciscans to found missions for this coastal tribe were not successful. Never large in numbers, the Karankawa population dwindled as a result of diseases contracted from Europeans. During the 19th century, many of the Indians were killed in warfare with Jean Lafitte's pirates and with Anglo-American colonists. Remaining members of the tribe fled to Mexico about 1843. Annihilation of that remnant about 1858 marked the disappearance of the Karankawa Indians.*

There is an Indian burial ground in Kleberg County, just south of Corpus Christi, that contained twenty skeletons when archaeologists excavated the site in 1927. The presence of burned bones could imply cannibalism or merely the practice of cremating their medicine men during a burial ceremony.

West of Corpus Christi on Highway 44 lies the town of Agua Dulce, which derives its name from the Spanish phrase for "sweet water," referring to a nearby creek. On March 2, 1836, a skirmish happened here during the Texas War of Independence, and its outcome was not so sweet. Two civilians, Dr. James Grant and Mr. Francis Johnson, raised a troop of volunteers to attack Mexico and take over the city of Matamoros. Two factors led to their mission's eventual demise: the disapproval of Sam Houston caused several of the recruits to abandon the endeavor, and the two "commanders" split their forces in order to hunt for livestock. When they encountered General Urrea and his reinforcement of three hundred Mexican foot soldiers, the Texans were inexperienced and scant in number. Among the group who camped at San Patricio, eighteen were killed and thirty-two captured, while Johnson was one of the five who escaped. At Agua Dulce Creek, Grant and twelve others were killed, while six were captured and six escaped.

Nearly ten years after Texas won its independence from Mexico, the United States military occupied the Corpus Christi area in order to solidify the implementation of Texas's statehood. During this time, the Artesian Park in Corpus Christi witnessed the presence of several prominent historical figures, like General Zachary Taylor. Another landmark you can visit within the city limits is the site of the old Corpus Christi lighthouse. As this area was beginning to thrive—once it was free from Mexican occupation and virtually all of the major Indian threats were pressed north into the plains—Colonel John Moore proposed plans for the construction of a harbor. In 1857, a brick lighthouse was erected, and its survival and function from that point on were precarious at best. It became a powder magazine during the Civil War, and eventually two anonymous Confederates orchestrated an explosion inside the structure so it would not fall into the grip of Union hands. By 1878, the city took the lighthouse down, as it was dilapidated and abandoned.

We took Highway 136 out of Corpus Christi, crossing through the town of Bayside at the Refugio County line. The cotton grows profusely along this road, and coupled with the quaintly pastel-colored houses and bay view decks, this route provides a wonderfully scenic drive. As you pass the Copano Bay, there is a historic marker for the old site of the town of Copano, named for the Copane Indians who originally inhabited the area. This location was a major port of entry for colonists (mainly Irish) and pirates alike for 150 years, from 1722 to 1870. The army of the Texas Revolution used it for its winter lodging in 1835. While the town itself was abandoned in the 1880s, Copano Bay today is alive and well, and there is abundant opportunity for fishing via both its State Fishing Pier and the more upscale Redfish Lodge resort, which operates year round and proclaims itself the "best kept secret" on the Gulf.

Highway 136 dead-ends into Highway 77 toward Refugio, and our historic tour of the Gulf coast continues there. Deriving its name from the mission Our Lady of Refuge, the last mission the Spanish built in Texas in 1795, Refugio was settled by Irish immigrants who were granted this area by the Mexican government. Because Refugio County was occupied by Mexico until Texas won its war for independence, it contains a few interesting locations that were sites of contention at the time, and it's worth a drive past these spots if you can envision what happened there. On Highway 77, fifteen miles south of Refugio, lies the location of General Jose Urrea's camp in 1836, now called Urrea Oaks. It was not until commanders Amon B. King and William Ward left their post at the Refugio Mission that Urrea was finally able to defeat the Texans in this region, and he lost a lot of men in the process. Upon his victory at Refugio, Urrea and his remaining men piled their dead comrades into a ditch four feet by four feet, making a pile as high as twenty cords of wood, according to one witness. This mass grave is known today as the Yucatan Soldiers' Burial Site.

Our historic drive continued from the Gulf coast to the southern plains region as we ventured into Goliad. This city was originally a part of Mexico's northern frontier, and the famous Mexican general Ignacio Zaragoza was born here. Inside Goliad State Park, there is a bronze statue of Zaragoza, celebrating the importance of this Mexican war hero who has been named the "Father of Cinco de Mayo." On May 5, 1862, he commanded a poorly equipped army against Napoleon's French forces at the Battle of Puebla. He made a speech that roused his troops, though they were less prepared and experienced, to defeat the French. "Your enemies are the first soldiers of the world, but you are the first sons of Mexico. They wish to seize your Fatherland, Soldiers! I read victory and faith on your foreheads. Long live Independence! Long live the Fatherland!" Today in Goliad, the General Zaragoza Society preserves and celebrates the memory of this inspiring figure.

Goliad, Texas, is perhaps most famous for the Espiritu Santo Mission, or Mission of the Holy Spirit. Spain built this mission and fortified it with the adjacent Presidio la Bahia because of external threats from France and domestic threats from hostile Indian tribes. The history of this structure is wrought with strife. It became the stage for revolution, and the players in one of its scenes unwittingly performed a harrowing tragedy. Colonel James Fannin and his troops occupied the Presidio during the Texas War of Independence, and like Ward and King, his retreat from the fort enabled Mexican General Urrea's eventual victory. At the Battle of Coleto, Fannin and his men negotiated the terms of their surrender, and they were taken back to the fort to be held prisoner. The captors from the previous battle at Refugio were combined with

La Bahia.

Fannin's men, making a total of 341 prisoners. At sunrise on March 27, 1836, Palm Sunday, those who could walk were taken out of the fort and massacred. Fannin and the others who were injured were murdered inside the fort. A total of 342 men were executed at the Goliad Massacre, and this incident incited the outrage of the Texans and portrayed the Mexican army under Santa Anna as outrageously sinister and cruel. A famous battle cry, "Remember the Alamo! Remember Goliad!" aroused the courage of those who fought and finally won their independence at San Jacinto.

From Goliad, Highway 59 passes through Fannin, where you can see the Fannin Battleground Historic Site, and then through Raisin, Texas, population fifty, on your way to Victoria, called the "Crossroads of South Texas." Like most of the towns in this region, it began as a Mexican colony and was occupied by Mexico until the Texas War of Independence ended in 1837. In August 1840, Victoria's townspeople experienced the wrath of Buffalo Hump and felt the sting of his revenge for the chiefs who were killed at the Council House Fight in San Antonio. Fehrenbach describes what happened when hundreds of Comanches surrounded this town:

Goliad Park.

The Comanches had already ridden around and surrounded the town of Victoria. Whooping warriors appeared out of the blue, taking the settlement by complete surprise, and cut down several luckless inhabitants on the outskirts. They killed a number of black slaves working in the fields. Had they ridden immediately into the town and been prepared to hunt down the whites on foot, there is little question that their hundreds could have slaughtered the entire population. But as always, this was not the Comanche way. Buffalo Hump's warriors circled the town like a bison stand, seizing horses and cattle, running down a small Negro child and carrying her away. And as always, such a medicine circle worked no magic against stout buildings. The walls stood, and the townspeople, alerted, had time to barricade their streets and houses.

The people of Victoria stayed behind cover while the Comanches mutilated the corpses of the dead, speared cattle, and rode around the outskirts in screeching triumph. The warriors kept up this game all day, and kept the town surrounded through the night. Then, on the 7th, when

Buffalo Hump persuaded some of his men to ride into the streets, attacking and setting fire to houses, the townsmen opened up with blistering fire from roofs and windows. Quickly losing stomach for a house-to-house search, the warriors retreated, driving off some two thousand mules and horses. One group of Mexican traders in the town lost five hundred head, and the Comanches had killed fifteen people at Victoria.

The Comanches' attack on Victoria was one incident in what came to be called the Linnville Raid. After the sack of Linnville, near Lavaca Bay on the coast, Buffalo Hump continued his revenge mission north to Caldwell County, where the Battle of Plum Creek took place. Here the Comanches lost all the loot they had gathered in Linnville and saw their revenge efforts squelched by an ardent Texas militia.

Passing through the site of the raid, we headed due north on Highway 77 into Lavaca County. French explorers first named the Lavaca River, calling it Les Veches, the cattle, for the abundance of buffalo covering the area. The Spanish retained the description, using the name La Baca, which eventually evolved into Lavaca. Highway 77 crosses through Hallettsville, the center of Lavaca County, which was settled by a female frontier "entrepreneur," Margaret Hallett. After her husband died in Goliad, Mrs. Hallett moved to the log cabin he built on the banks of the Lavaca River and set up a small store, and the others soon built houses around her.

Next we drove through Schulenberg in Fayette County, a colorful little town combining the icons of Catholicism with country flavor. A family "smokehouse" along the highway draws its crowd with the sign "Come as U R Bring Ma n Pa." A little farther north lies La Grange where, outside the main town, the road curves around great hills, and large houses with wooded lawns decorated our drive. A roadside marker in La Grange reveals a spot replete with sentimentality. It designates not merely the type of common war memorial that reminds us of citizens who sacrificed their lives, but it is also a more personal place where troops convened to rally behind their cause and speak their goodbyes. The roadside marker for Fayette County's historic oak reads:

It was under this historic oak when the men of Capt. Nicholas Mosby Dawson's company assembled on September 15, 1842 and went to the relief of San Antonio to repel the invasion of Texas by the Mexican

Army under Gen. Adrian Woll. In the fight near Salado Creek, September 18, Dawson and 35 of his men were killed, 15 captured and imprisoned in Castle Perote in Mexico, and 3 escaped. Here on the courthouse square, the scarred remains of what was once a mighty oak marks the spot from which La Grange has on every occasion sent its sons to battle. In fights with the Indians, the struggle with Mexico, in the War Between the States, the Spanish American War, and in two World Wars, sons of Fayette County were first marshaled under this tree. Wives, mothers, sweethearts here bade farewell and sent their men to battle, each time to win acclaim as true patriots.

To me, it is remarkable that the people of this area have preserved the "scarred remains" of what was once "mighty" in the simple location of an oak tree. This marker strikes me as a testament to their pride and reverence for those who now, like the oak, exist only in the writings of history.

Lee County's pioneers, who were mostly Czech and German, could tell us today of Indians who were both friendly and treacherous. On November 26, 1836, Indians murdered the first white settler of Lee County, James Goucher (sometimes spelled "Gotier"), and four of his family members—his wife, son-in-law and two sons. You can drive past their graves, just four miles south of Giddings. In Lexington, right along Highway 77, is a spot that was once a favorite Indian campsite, at which an old buffalo trail intersected a branch of Yegua Creek. In 1837, a band of Tonkawa Indians camped here, and San Jacinto veteran James Shaw honored their kindness and hospitality to the white settlers by naming the place Indian Camp Branch.

The Tonkawas were the first known occupants of Lee County, and they were typically friendly to the whites. Ironically, they also fell prey to the Comanches, arguably the most formidable opponent Texas has ever seen.

Crossing the
Red/Fort Sill

In Fort Worth in December, the weather can be capricious. There may be a snap so sharp it sends the mercury plummeting from sixty-four to fourteen and the previously green leaves of the pecan trees simultaneously free-falling to their inevitable destiny. As a result of just such a cold snap, I once watched as the tree in my backyard showered every single leaf it had in a matter of five minutes, covering the icy ground with a dry, shaggy blanket. The winter weather blast was upon us, dubbed so by the local news. In Fort Worth in December, you may find people hunkered down under scarves and furry hats, as well as the rest of the ski wear they rarely get to use, just to grab the basics at the grocery store and get back home. Others shiver in a slow and slumped gait, while perky dogs on the ends of their leashes exuberantly relish the unexpected frost. But in Fort Worth in December, these conditions are not always the case.

On this particular twentieth day of the month, for instance, it was one of those no-jacket-required, "is it really the first day of winter tomorrow?" kinds of days, which in Rick's estimation means a good day for a road trip. Camera packed and sunglasses on, we headed northwest.

Following a route we knew all too well, we took Highway 199 into Jacksboro, where Fort Richardson sits on about three hundred acres just a half-mile south of the main town on a tributary of the Trinity. It is estimated that the entire construction of the fort, fifty-five buildings at its largest, cost the United States $800,000. Richardson was a busy place

The Fort Richardson cannon.

in the 1800s because it was the farthest north of the Texas forts and 120 miles away from Fort Sill in Oklahoma. We usually take the Cadillac on a loop through the fort, and it's a great, shaded, usually quiet place to get out and walk around. It's now a state park, so Fort Richardson would also be an inviting place to camp out or fish that is not too far from the sprawling Dallas/Fort Worth metroplex. At least once a year, they restock the waters with catfish and trout.

Jacksboro is the first place I visited with Rick when we started taking road trips together. That first time we came through town, he took me into the Dairy Queen where, in an alcove of the main dining area, there are a few framed prints of the first Indian chiefs to be tried in the whites' court of law, and Rick told me, with an expression acknowledging that the information need not be pointed out, that these Kiowa chiefs were found guilty on all counts. However, because every trial begins with an indictment, the tale begins earlier than that, at Fort Sill, where General Sherman first placed the chiefs under arrest, and even before that, back near Jacksboro, at the scene of the original crime. So our day trip across the Red River from Fort Worth and back home again actually works to tell a famous story of how the mighty reign of the Comanches and Kiowas came slowly unraveling to its end.

By the 1860s, the Kiowa tribes were weakened by a distinct lack of unity after their leader, Dohasan, or Little Mountain, died—then several, instead of one, inherited his position. Two of these new chiefs, Satank and Satanta, attended the Medicine Lodge council up in Kansas, where they signed a treaty agreeing to move to the reservation near Fort Sill in Oklahoma and leave Texas exclusively to peaceful white settlement. Thus the Red River rivalry was born, and I imagine that the chiefs were never sorrier than they were to have signed that proverbial piece of paper. Restless and miserable on his new reservation, and fueled with a desire to avenge his son's murder in Texas, Satank joined forces with Satanta, gathered Big Tree and a few other Comanche and Kiowa warriors and ventured south into the forbidden Texas territory that used to be theirs.

Enter onto the stage a few truly memorable characters, like Satank, the muscular, debonair Kiowa chief with a distinguished, Spanish-looking moustache. Old Satank was bitter with grief at the loss of those days when the Kiowas freely hunted and camped at will, and maybe this sentiment for the loss of time and power manifested itself in his extraordinary grief for the death of his son, reportedly killed while on a raid in Texas. The suicidal Satank rode alongside a separate pony, which bore his son's meticulously packed bones.

Next there was Satanta, the intelligent orator who learned to play the white military's bugle calls and who had previously sacrificed to the sun four deep gashes of flesh from his back in order to receive a sacred shield, thus respected by whites for the very same reasons he was feared. In fact, the *New York Times* maintained this dual fascination with Satanta throughout his reign, printing in 1867 that "in cunning or native diplomacy Satanta has no equal in boldness, daring and merciless cruelty."

A prominent figure in the Kiowa raiding season of 1871 was Maman-ti, or Sky Walker, a medicine man toting a stuffed owl with button eyes, which revealed prophesies from the voices of Kiowas past. Not a chief, the Owl Prophet, as he came to be known, operated behind the scenes, prophesying when and where the Kiowas should attack for the best fortune or good medicine. It was this prophet who led the raid that took the life of Britt Johnson earlier that year. One of the very few men of color to have become famous during this time, Johnson courageously faced the Indians to negotiate the ransom of white captives, and he was known and revered in the frontier for this feat.

There was a whole slew of others, whose names imply what their costumes and mannerisms would be, should we actually perform this play. Enter Kicking Bird, Yellow Wolf, Gun Shot, Eagle Heart and the young, tough guy, Big Tree, among many others totaling somewhere between 100 and 150. The many accounts of this alliance's raid all compare from a distance, but zoom in the camera lens and the details change quite a bit.

Here's where the first act, set just a few miles outside of Jacksboro, begins. Our band of raiders headed into Texas looking for trouble. The Owl Prophet consulted his oracle, frozen except for the occasional ruffling of its feathers as the breeze came and went. This symbol of death and a portal into the spirit world told him that two separate caravans were headed past Salt Creek Prairie, right where the warriors camped in Jack County. Voices of the dead instructed the Kiowa chiefs to leave the first group of travelers unharmed, for their reward rode somehow with the second caravan.

The first, unbeknownst to our war party, happened to be General William T. Sherman on his way to Fort Richardson; ironically, he was in the process of appraising the "situation" on the Texas frontier. When he reached the fort, Sherman commented that, from his observations, the whites were safer than they'd ever been. Women and children ventured about unarmed and seemingly with an air of security, "as though they were in Illinois," which they surely would not do if they actually feared any uninvited visitors. But while Sherman cast a perfunctory glance here and there, surveying what looked like a peaceful prairie scene, fiery eyes, hot with a fever of vengeance and antsy with anticipation for what would follow, covertly watched him pass.

The next to pass was a wagon train of teamsters led by Captain Henry Warren, carting loads of corn from fort to fort. The Kiowa chiefs and their band descended on these unsuspecting men with a fervor fueled by the restlessness spawned by their fenced-in days on the reservation but also fueled by Owl Prophet's omen—attacking this second group would produce wondrous medicine. So attack they did. Imagine the scene acted out. The *clip-clop* of horse hooves leisurely keeps the tempo constant while the wagons' passengers, oblivious to the horrors coming their way, hum, chew tobacco or tell jokes. Suddenly, a silence as frozen as death takes over when they first hear the distinctive squeak of a leather saddle caused by a warrior atop a nearby hill straightening his posture to poise his lance above his head. At the sight of this warrior, the one chewing tobacco swallows hard. Other warriors slowly emerge, and in a split second the teamsters know what they're in for—pain.

In a whirlwind of total chaos, the Kiowa and Comanche men fly in from all directions. Imagine being the audience of this short tragedy, unable to blink your eyes as you witness the noisy violence of wooden crates toppling, wagon wheels rolling waywardly off into the wings, war ponies snorting and stamping the ground as their charges aim lances and bows and whooping Indians deftly exacting bloody, fatal blows on whites too startled to plan a strategy.

One teamster, Samuel Elliott, allegedly suffered long before he died. The Indians strapped him to an axle, or a wagon wheel as some accounts describe it, and slowly roasted him over a fire. A few escaped and were able to tell Sherman of the horrors they'd endured, forcing him to revisit his appraisal of safety in the Texas plains. The attack on the Warren wagon train that day renewed terror in the whites who lived scattered throughout the plains—if the presence of the area's forts and the natives' removal to Oklahoma had ever, as Sherman assumed, actually suppressed their fears to begin with. My assumption is that, as is sometimes the case even these days, the powers that be did not always have their finger on the pulse of the goings-on of common frontier folk, and they definitely didn't know how fearful it could be at times to live there out in the open range.

This drive along 199 toward the Red River would have been splattered with blood for acres and acres; so many skirmishes, seizures and sacrileges happened along the way. After Jacksboro, 199 becomes 281; northwest becomes due north, and there is not a lot to see along the roadside other than the ghosts of battles past; and endless fields checkered with oil rigs line both sides. In the fall, you'll spot camouflaged dove hunters and Labradors in these fields, but on this sunny December day, we were significantly alone.

In order to get across the Red and to our destination in mind, we flew on through Archer County, where in 1837 blood christened this segment of our trail, as well. On the Salt Fork of the Trinity, about ten miles south of Windthorst, seventeen or eighteen Texas Rangers broke away from their group—which was presumably on a scouting mission of little action and no consequence enough to suit its daredevil lust for adventure— and they headed toward the rock mounds known as the Stone Houses. Lieutenant Van Benthusen led the way northward. It didn't take long for the lieutenant to spot a trail of Indians, so his rangers followed the tracks. Unfortunately, these tracks did not belong to the Kichai (often "Keechi") horse thieves the full ranger company had originally pursued but rather to a friendly band of Cherokees and Delawares who were led by a Kichai guide. The lieutenant's men shot first and asked questions later, however, and they killed the friendly band's Kichai guide. Actually, it was a hotheaded Irishman, Felix McClusky, who killed this guide, ignoring his target's desperate motions indicating friendship. When his colleagues protested, he claimed again and again that he'd kill an Indian for a mere "plug of tobacco," and he produced a visual aid from his pocket, presumably pilfered from the Indian he'd just attacked.

Even in the rather remote conditions of the prairie, news traveled fast, and soon close to 150 Kichai Indians awaited Van Benthusen's crew, ready for a fight. In the first few seconds of this grossly disproportionate match, with no time for witty repartee, the rangers faced an angry mob, outnumbering them a whopping 10 to 1. Some say that 4 died in the two hours that composed the initial phase of the battle—others say 5. Regardless, once the number of rangers was cut by one-third, the Indians set fire to the prairie right in front of the ravine where the Texans concealed themselves and fired their arms. The rangers saw no choice but to retreat into the woods, and they lost 6 more of their men in this process. Accounts say that 8 to 10 miraculously survived the ordeal, but even after the battle, their wayward actions brought them once again right up to the threshold of death, as they had to travel on foot all the way back to the present-day Fort Worth area with sticky, stinging wounds, tattered clothing and angry, hungry stomachs. I wonder at what point the lieutenant regretted having separated from the original company. My "I told you so" moment would have happened much earlier, when McClusky jumped a guy as if he were starting a mere barroom brawl.

Even if the sight of pastures as far as you can see makes for a boring ride in the car, or even if the rhythmic and relentless turn of a pump jack puts you into an incurable trance, I would argue that there's still a good handful of reasons to do this drive, other than the rewards that await on the other side of the Red River. The fact is that these parts saw a lot of action in a pretty large chunk of time during Texas's frontier era, so I just ignore the lazy flatness of the present day, close my eyes and watch the violent tug-of-war match transpire.

Just another notch farther northward on our way into Wichita Falls, we crossed the Little Wichita River, where such a match did transpire: Kiowa chief Kicking Bird fought McClellan and the Sixth Cavalry here in 1870. The relocation to the reservation did a number on his spirit, too; like Satanta, Kicking Bird needed to get out of his fenced-in yard and fight. He gathered a huge band of Comanche and Kiowa warriors, about 250 according to most sources, and crossed the Red into Texas. Salt Creek Prairie was the location, coincidentally just months before Satanta's attack on the wagon train. Kicking Bird's men first wreaked chaos by trashing the stage station located close by and destroying the bags of mail stored there. McClellan found the scene of the robbery first, and then he followed Kicking Bird's trail.

Exquisitely armed and decorated, the Kiowa and Comanche warriors were not easy opponents. Reports claim that they carried Spencer rifles, which were breech-loaded and contained a six-shot magazine, making them far faster and easier to reload than the Sixth Cavalry's less fashionable ammo. Even so, McClellan's men suffered only two casualties and a few wounds and were able to retreat back to Fort Richardson. These overwhelming odds and the unbelievable outcome won thirteen of his men Medals of Honor. I guess we could call the Battle of the Little Wichita a win on both sides, since almost all of McClellan's men survived and Kicking Bird was able to save face when he returned to the reservation a less passive man.

Kicking Bird and Satanta and company all crossed the Red and returned to Oklahoma with the blood of whites on their hands, and they probably believed they did so with impunity. As we crossed the Red River, I noticed a hazy view of the Wichita Mountains to the northwest. I've always called ranges like these, which are so far off in the distance, "ghost mountains" because of their smoky borders and faint hues. They're like ethereal specters way out there, hardly physical matter when you compare them to their nearer, sharp-edged, hard and impervious counterparts. So there the mountains of the spirit world loomed up ahead as we made our grand entrance across the state line.

For card-carrying citizens of the Lone Star state, entering Oklahoma is contentious business. Crossing the Red means your beers will be weaker, and some find it unbearable to suffer the cacophony of cheers and the barrage of banners and bumper stickers for that football team that occasionally embarrasses the Longhorns. But being neither a person who drinks much beer nor one who invests much interest in college sports rivalries, I thought instead about the Comanches who begrudgingly agreed to go north of the Red, to the land "reserved" for their use and packaged nicely with promises of autonomy and peace from white expansion. Whenever we've driven through the Hill Country or whenever we cross under the cool canopy of trees in the thick of the Cross Timbers on Silver Creek Road, Rick often says, "It's no wonder the Indians fought so hard to keep their land." Crossing the Red River that sunny Saturday and seeing the first few yards of the unimpressive landscape of plain old Oklahoma created a response in me that is inversely proportionate to Rick's, and that response was, invariably, "It's no wonder the Indians fought so hard to keep their land."

While I am not native to Texas, it is becoming apparent to me that riding shotgun with Rick for these past few months has created a, dare I say it, geocentrism that precludes any possibility for a positive appraisal of other states. Thus, on this unseasonably warm December day, when Rick decided that we'd get in the car and go north, I looked forward to getting out of the house and to our inaugural visit to a currently operational military fort, but I did not know that Oklahoma also held a covert treasure, just two and a half hours from my front door. But first, we went to Fort Sill.

The historic events on September 11, 2001, created a new protocol for entering a fully operating military fort. At various times, we've been asked to raise Fort DeVille's hood, open all doors, produce identification and even show proof of car insurance and registration. So, with a little apprehension, we approached Fort Sill, knowing that we were at its mercy, and no tap dance or balancing act could be too far from the imagination. We succumbed to the search, which was far less extensive, by the way, than the one we more recently suffered at Fort Leavenworth, and we headed into the grounds.

Both historic and modern buildings stand in the complex, and it didn't take us long to spot the Sherman house, which was simply and tastefully

The Sherman House.

decorated with red-ribboned wreaths for Christmas. We stopped here specifically because of the old narrative our day trip was reconstructing. The bloody deeds the fields along 199 bore witness to also culminated here when, on the porch of the fort's commanding officer, Brevet Major General Benjamin Grierson, Sherman arrested Satank, Satanta and Big Tree for their theft of forty-one mules and their murder of the Warren wagon train's teamsters.

Unaware, or perhaps indifferent, that the news of their bloody acts preceded them, Satanta and the others returned to the reservation to collect their Saturday rations. When the reservation's Quaker agent, Lawrie Tatum, interrogated him, Satanta readily claimed responsibility for the raid, and Satank and the others enthusiastically nodded in agreement. Among other grievances, Satanta told Agent Tatum that the Indians had been "taken by the hair and pulled here close to the Texans where we have to fight." The chiefs were then brought before the general of the U.S. Army, William Tecumseh Sherman, who declared Satank,

Satanta and Big Tree under arrest at Fort Sill, and when the possibility of their resistance reared its ugly head, the noses of many carbines eased their way out of the windows of Grierson's house, just in case the chiefs saw a need to hear the severity of these charges reiterated.

Attempts to intervene on their behalf were squelched. Kicking Bird tried to secure their freedom by promising to pay the restitution immediately (forty-one mules) and to keep a better eye on the warriors who were clearly afflicted with a wanderlust made worse by their prolonged residence on the reservation. Lone Wolf showed up with a couple of carbines and bows, but he was of course no match for the troops positioned there.

A few days later, their means of extradition arrived, and the chiefs were loaded into a wagon and brought, manacled, to Texas. The reservation's schoolteacher made a note that the main difference in the attitudes of the three prisoners was a direct function of their age: Big Tree, at twenty-two, was "anxious to live"; Satanta, at fifty, did not care either way; and Satank, seventy years old, would rather die than go to trial in Texas. And he was able to bring about his desired fate soon enough, because he rode in a separate wagon, chanting his death song while concealed under a blanket. Old Satank had told a fellow tribesman to look for his body beside a certain tree along the way to Fort Richardson, and in a spooky turn of events, he was able to make that very thing happen. Separated from Satanta and Big Tree, he rode in the front wagon; he desperately chewed through his hand so that he could slip out of his manacles. He reached for one of the guards' weapons but was shot in the chest during the scuffle. The men left his body propped against a tree, just as he promised it would be, and they conveyed the other two without incident into Texas.

Grierson's house came to be named the Sherman House, and for our particular interests, it was the landmark we didn't want to miss while we toured Fort Sill that Saturday. We also cruised slowly past old barracks, a corral, officers' quarters and the museum and store. Filled with books and memorabilia of all kind, this well-kept little shop is worth getting out of the car for, and we left there loaded down with pens, t-shirts and souvenirs galore. And so Fort Sill came and went for me, and I was already starting to revisit my prejudicial notions about Oklahoma. It was an interesting place to me because of the old story and the unprecedented arrests of those unsuspecting chiefs. But it also had my attention because there were current military operations afoot, and in December 2003 we had all caught a little of the fever of patriotism—that kind of intangible force acted over us that made most of us just a little friendlier, a little more polite and a little bit less self-absorbed, knowing that there were nineteen-year-olds running an endless number of quarter-mile laps and doing push-ups nearby so they could dodge explosions and operate mighty tanks much farther away.

We left Fort Sill to pursue our next Oklahoma interest, one that Rick had seen many, many times but that remained a mystery to me. We headed just a few miles north on I-44 and west on Highway 49 into the Wichita Mountains and finally spotted our turnoff—the one leading to Mount Scott. My jaw dropped open as I looked up to see a car spiraling its way up the huge rock, turned to Rick and asked, "Is that what we were looking for?" On www.peakbagger.com, one climbing enthusiast whose photograph appears on the site calls Mount Scott a "huge surprise"; here's a peak in Oklahoma that looks like a "real mountain." Rising a whopping 2,464 feet above sea level, it is real—colorful, too.

Rick deftly worked Fort DeVille around those hairpin curves (it's drivable; I've since returned in a Ford F-150) up the three-and-a-half-mile paved road to the summit, where you can park your vehicle and explore by foot. We stepped out to the kind of crisp breeze that tugs at your hair and shouts in your ear, which means only one thing: water is nearby. From our vantage point, we could see bright blue Lake Elmer Thomas, just sparsely populated that day with about three sailboats. I'm afraid I have to admit that, compared to a few of Texas's brown reservoirs I've spotted from the window of an airplane, this clean water was a cool relief to my eyes.

Once I got my bearings and got acclimated to the height, I noticed Mount Scott's intricacies—namely, the continuous swirls of pink, orange and gray that decorate this massive rock, like it's been worked on by nature's graffiti artist. My research has led me to only a vague explanation of these vibrant colors that grace the whole breadth and height of this mountain—that it's covered with some kind of moss and algae. I guess the nearby water and the temperature and moisture level in the air make just the right conditions for this combination of colorful "paints." Whatever the explanation, it's really beautiful. It's like studying a giant work of art, one in which the brush strokes and shades vary enough to keep you occupied all day. And we all prefer this

Mount Scott.

A flower at Mount Scott.

kind of graffiti to the alternative: the crumbled Doritos bags, crushed-flat beer cans, silver pop tops, rolled-up dirty diapers and even an occasional tennis shoe that now grace the crevices and ledges in once pristine Turner Falls. Once again, I stood here taking pictures and gazing around this prize, and my appraisal of Oklahoma was revisited, to say the least.

When we'd had enough of the wind, we wound our way back down the mountain and drove into Medicine Park, Oklahoma's "Historic Cobblestone Community," to look for a place to eat lunch. Senator Elmer Thomas, the namesake of Mount Scott's lake, founded Medicine Park on the Fourth of July 1908. The local Indian tribes actually first used the term "medicine" to describe the area's mystic powers. Before Fort Sill developed, it was a tiny military camp, Camp Wichita, referred to by the Indians as "the soldier house at Medicine Bluffs." The water that ran along Medicine Park's prospective town site was Medicine Creek, which they believed had healing powers. This tiny town was built, therefore, as a resort and health spa, and it successfully generated tourism, but it also unexpectedly drew people in as permanent residents. Pretty soon, the wealthy and distinguished were rubbing elbows with the reckless and notorious; during Prohibition times, for example, the little cobblestone village housed card games, slot machines, billiards and plenty of liquor. I have no trouble imagining the spirits of all kinds that flow freely through this place, and they have flown since before its buildings ever existed.

Rick and I drove around for a while; it doesn't take long to get through Medicine Park, but there's a lot to take in. We took a picture of some really impressive metal sculptures on display in someone's front yard. We crossed the main bridge over the creek, spotting several footbridges within the ravine. We passed the swimming hole, a dammed-up portion of Medicine Creek officially called Bath Lake. I'm sure shopping attracts most of today's tourists, and I wrote down some of the shop names because I couldn't believe how diverse a place this was. At first I wanted to call it "artsy" but then "hippie" came to mind, and then I saw all the bikes and their leather-clad riders. Rusty Buffalo, The Laughing Lizard, The Purple Parrot, Charley's Angel, Chaps My Ass…you can see what I mean. The important thing, though, is that the character of this little town truly can't be defined. And forget about stereotypes. I imagine that as soon as you settled on one, somebody would walk right in and shatter it. I love that about Medicine Park. Anybody fits in here, it seems to me.

We fit right in at the Riverside Café, where we ate lunch right along the edge of Medicine Creek. It wasn't too crowded; of course, Rick and I eat our meals at unconventional hours, partly to avoid noontime crowds but mostly because when we finally do stop, we've been holding out until we could find something unique and "worthy" in our eyes.

From the café we retraced our tracks all the way home, out of Oklahoma and into Wichita Falls, where train tracks and oil refineries reign supreme. The town declares itself "Home of the Hotter-n-Hell Hundred," an annual bicycle race that's one of the largest of its kind. What we saw when we came through town was a spectacle all its own. On the lawn at Midwestern State University, what looked like parade floats carting Christmas lights made sparkles and trails of color while we slowed down the car to take some pictures. What we got on film were dizzy smears of color, but the overall effect is there all the same. People walked along the circular drive, while the parade of lights twirled around and around the lawn to rote music like a giant unceasing carousel. Having spent a good bit of his life in Wichita Falls, Rick explained that the spectacle began as Mrs. Burns's private display of Christmas decorations, and the thing got so big that they eventually moved it to the campus; those magic lights and music became a tradition for the whole town.

One short anecdote from Wichita Falls' history reveals the effectiveness and efficiency of the citizens' actions—the bank robbery of 1896. It involved two horseback outlaws, Elmer "Kid" Lewis and Foster Crawford, whose names sound perfect for characters in an old western. The two robbed a bank, were apprehended and jailed by rangers and were taken out in front of the scene of the crime and lynched, all in a span of a mere twenty-four hours. Those Christmas lights added just the right touch to an otherwise unseasonably warm day. It was after dark when we left Wichita Falls to finish our route home.

However, the story wouldn't be complete without telling the fate of Satanta and Big Tree after they arrived in Jacksboro for their trial, and it's fitting that we end it here, as we crossed back through Jacksboro on our way home. At their indictment at the Fort Richardson Courthouse, the charges were the following: the two chiefs murdered seven teamsters "with force and malice and not having the fear of God before their eyes, but being moved and seduced by the instigation of the devil." Thus began the *State of Texas v. Satanta and Big Tree*, and such a trial was never seen in this country, nor, for that matter, will one like it ever be seen again.

Judge Charles Soward from Weatherford presided over the trial in a hot July Texas courtroom in 1871. Both sides made compelling arguments; the jury deliberated briefly, and they returned with a verdict of guilty, sentencing the chiefs to hang until they are "dead, dead, dead!" The chiefs were held under heavy guard at Fort Richardson, surely to protect them from vigilante justice, which would predictably have been more gruesome and sadistic than anything the Wichita Falls bank robbers suffered. It would be the lynching to end all lynchings. Before they could be executed, however, Texas governor Edmund Davis lessened their sentences to life imprisonment, after some urging from Agent Tatum. Of course, this "leniency" was quite controversial, but the governor was convinced that it would help future relations with the Indians on the reservation if their chiefs were not killed. The chiefs spent a couple of years in Huntsville before their inevitable release became a key bargaining chip in white/Indian negotiations. By September 1873, they were back at the Wichita Reservation near Fort Sill.

North and south and back again, across the Red they went, held accountable by a foreign culture's legal system, which, when the yo-yo stopped spinning, ultimately spared them their lives. I still like hearing Rick tell the story of the chiefs who were tried in the white man's court, and I still like going to the Dairy Queen just to see those dusty pictures, but now I also like a few things about Oklahoma. The best part is that the whole trip spans no more than six hours, at a leisurely pace.

Texas Forts Trail

I once read in Annie Dillard's *Pilgrim at Tinker Creek* that the Indians carved grooves into their arrow shafts, so that the blood from an animal pierced, but not slain, could stream down the arrow and paint a trail on the ground for the hunter to follow. The Indian "lightning mark" is a smart, simple invention that creates an unmistakable path of evidence leading eventually to the honored prize of food or fur.

On the Texas frontier in the mid-1800s, the Indians who had been here for thousands of years and the whites who had traveled hundreds of long, grueling miles in large caravans from the eastern states fought for possession of the open range. Both parties had bellicose, courageous spirits that would not allow them to forfeit their claim, which was a virtual paradise of wild game, an abundance of water, mountains and prairies. This road trip focuses on the war itself, passing both of the actual forts built to house the troops and supplies needed to defeat the passionate Comanches and the less renowned places where particular citizens confronted small groups of Indians. In some way, for me, following the Texas Forts Trail was like drawing back a mighty bow and shooting a mystic arrow back through time. We traced this route like the Indian archer would follow a trail of blood, to discover its source, however vicious or tame.

We started out of Fort Worth going west on I-20 through Weatherford. We picked up the Forts Trail at Highway 16, heading north through

Strawn. With a population of 694, Strawn boasts the work of a range of artisans, from soap and candle makers to metal sculptors. It was early on a Saturday morning when we drove through town, and we stopped to take a few pictures of the bronze sculptures set on display just outside the main square. There was a giant armadillo that spanned at least fifteen feet and a cleverly assembled dung beetle, in its characteristic handstand formation, working hard to roll a giant ball with its back legs. Unique culture abounds in this town, though its residents appear to sleep late. We didn't see a single soul entering or exiting the shops, and the well-known Mary's Café was closed.

Strawn lies in Palo Pinto County, an area thick with stories of encounters with Indians. Our drive north on Highway 16 passes right through the area where W.J. Hale twice fought with Indians. In 1871, according to Hale himself, Indians ambushed him as he made his way to Palo Pinto. Just as he crossed Ioni Creek, the air was suddenly filled with arrows sailing toward him. He had a six-shooter on either side, and he fired them both as he ran. A little farther eastward, he was finally able to fend them off with a few shots from his Winchester. Apparently, in those days, if you were to occupy the same land as the Comanche warrior, you didn't venture far from home without adequate ammunition. Hale survived another skirmish in 1872, just nine miles northeast of Strawn. The Indians surrounded him, and he fired upon them, striking their leader. They quickly fled, and Hale was once again able to scramble to safety.

Like Hale, a young ranch hand named Fred Colley was attacked by several Indians where Highway 16 intersects at Highway 180, just a few miles west of Palo Pinto. He was riding a good horse, so he attempted to outrun them. Joseph Carroll McConnell describes the final scene of Colley's life in his book *The West Texas Frontier*:

> *During his dash for life, an Indian with his bow and arrows, gave Colley a mortal wound.* [He] *pulled the arrow from his body and used it to whip his horse. When he reached the fence of the Dodson Ranch, after running about two miles, young Colley fell dead.*

Another famous murder that happened along Ioni Creek was Jesse Veale's. In his book *Goodbye to a River*, John Graves describes what he imagines might have happened the day Jesse Veale and his friend, Joe

The giant bronze armadillo.

The bronze dung beetle sculpture.

Corbin, stole a few of the Indians' horses, left unattended in a grove of cedar:

> *"Jesse," Joe Corbin said, "they's two Indians a-lookin' at us from on top of that bank. They's more than two..."*
>
> *Afoot, likely because it had been their ponies the boys had taken upriver, the Comanches began to shoot, and an arrow hit Jesse Veale in the knee, and his horse went to bucking off to one side. Joe Corbin yelled: "What the hell we gonna do?"*
>
> *Jesse yelled something back. To Joe Corbin it sounded like: "Run it out!" He did, snapping his useless pistol at an Indian who tried to grab his reins and ducked aside from the misfire, lashing his pony on up the bank's rise... When he last looked back (how many times did he see it again, the rest of his life, how many times did he wonder if what Jesse Veale had said was "Fight it out"?), Jesse was on the ground shooting and clubbing with his pistol, and they were all over him. And when Joe Corbin came back with help from a ranch not far away, they found Jesse Veale sitting dead but unscalped against a double-elm tree, his pistol gone, Comanche blood on the ground around him.*

Both Indians and whites lost their lives, avenging the theft of horses or the murder of ones honored and loved. In an endless chain of revenge, it seems that neither side allowed the other to have the last victory.

We turned west on Highway 180 and witnessed a stark transformation in the landscape. A low road, slicing a path through the Palo Pinto Mountains, Highway 180 is lined on either side with only cedar, cacti and rock, and it looks like it hasn't changed significantly since the time of the old frontier. The blood-soaked banks of Ioni Creek and the bones found at Metcalf Gap could testify to the violence of the era, proving that survival on Texas land came at no small price.

In this area of our drive otherwise devoid of the seasonal fiery reds and oranges, the town of Caddo arises, named for the colorful Caddo Indian tribe, who dominated the eastern Texas frontier for hundreds of years. At the junction of Highway 180 and Farm Road 717 lies the historical marker for Caddo; the town was settled just a few miles from the place along Caddo Creek where its namesake Indian tribe resided.

The majority of the Caddos lived in east Texas and parts of Louisiana, with the greatest concentration of people around Nacogdoches. They had a farming culture, and they gained the respect of French and Spanish explorers, who admired their artful pottery and attractive clothing.

Highway 180 west leads to Breckenridge, and on the day we drove through, the townspeople ate their Saturday morning breakfasts with at least one eye peering out the window, the mark of anticipation for the annual Christmas Parade. Inside Peg & Greg's Café, the patrons were attired in red sweatshirts and sweaters, sparkling with appliqués of teddy bears and rocking horses. Inside comfortable shoes, they wore socks with bells that jingled. We stopped to eat, but we settled for coffee because the waitress was remarkably preoccupied with the coming of the parade. She was pleased to report, when we sat down in a booth by the window, that we had the "best seats in the house."

We continued west on 180 across the bridge at Hubbard Creek Lake and turned north on Highway 283 at the town of Albany, heading toward Fort Griffin State Park. During the time of the Indian wars, Fort Griffin served as a center of operations for the military. After a few years of conflict, the Indians moved farther west, and the area surrounding Fort Griffin was rendered safe for white settlers. Now the park provides facilities for camping and hiking and serves as residence for a herd of Texas longhorns. Fort Griffin was situated on top of a hill, and a town of the same name developed in the bottomland between the hill and the clear fork of the Brazos River. What came to be known as the Flats quickly gained a reputation for lawlessness, and it attracted such famous outlaws as "The Poker Queen" Lottie Deno, Mollie McCabe and John Wesley Hardin. The most famous of law enforcers also spent some time in the Flats, specifically Doc Holliday, Wyatt Earp and Patrick F. Garrett. In Albany, we drove past the Hereford Motel, a modern rendition of the Flats, with awnings bearing old names such as "Lottie's" and "The Beehive Saloon." Nearby, a sign hailed us as we drove through town: "Visitors Y'all Are the Greatest!"

The prominent color scheme on Highway 283 was that of dry hay and the rust of corrugated metal, usually partially serving as the walls and roof for an old barn or shed. The absence of green in the view of a landscape always seems to get my attention because it isn't what we've come to expect. Green grass and blue skies, the rudimentary elements of

Wendi at Fort Griffin.

nature, are easier to imagine out there along the roadside, but a palette of only sepia shades looks like the artificial creation of a painter.

Continuing to watch the landscape play tricks on the mind on the way out of Albany, we headed farther west on Highway 180 until we passed a highway marker that read "8.6 Miles South to Fort Phantom Hill." We decided to try our luck, so we turned south onto County Road 329, zigzagging through pastures on a rough gravel road for about six miles and eventually coming out at Highway 600, just two miles from the fort. In *Along the Texas Forts Trail*, Aston and Taylor provide two explanations for how this fort came to be called "Phantom Hill":

> *On approaching the post you will see the remaining chimneys standing like sentinels on what looks like a formidable hill overlooking the clear Fork of the Brazos. As one nears the hill it disappears and becomes a gentle slope, barely perceptible when one arrives; thus one of the stories of how the post got its name. A second account has to do with a nervous*

sentry firing on what he thought was an Indian on the hill. A following investigation failed to discover the presence of any Indians, and one of the troopers suggested that the man had seen a ghost.

Although a few of the old buildings still stand, and they are visible from the road, Fort Phantom Hill has no entrance to the public, even for a walk through the grounds. When Phantom Hill was first built, the times spent there were characterized mostly by hardship. The men stationed at the fort did not see any major Indian battles: "The only break in the monotony of fort life was excursions into the field, which meant extended marches across arid land with inadequate supplies of food and water."

As you drive past Fort Phantom Hill, Highway 600 south will take you through Abilene along the Forts Trail to 277 south. In this segment of the trip, it's worth slowing down to gaze out the window. The horizon on either side is lush green and mountainous. Turn off at Farm Road 1235, where a sign points the way to Buffalo Gap 7 miles ahead. Named for the prolific amounts of buffalo that passed through a "gap" in the Callahan Divide, this area was frequently traveled by Indians, buffalo hunters and even Spanish explorers in earlier centuries because there was water and an abundance of game.

At the entrance to the Historic Village, we browsed through an elaborate gift shop and museum, whose clerks and tour guides all wore the costumes of the frontier period. Aston and Taylor describe this picturesque stop in *Along the Texas Forts Trail*:

> *Today visitors to Buffalo Gap will still find it a village nestled among the oaks. The two-story county jail constructed of native stone blocks and mortised together with cannonballs brought from Civil War battlefields stands as an anchor in the Buffalo Gap Historic Village...It is one of the best locally developed historic sites in the state. Dr. [Lee] Rode has collected such buildings as a doctor's and dentist's office, a railroad depot, a log cabin, a country church (which is used by many young people for their weddings), print shops, and barns filled with all types of western relics such as wagons.*

What caught my eye when we arrived at Buffalo Gap was the collage of images that decorated the entrance to the village. There was a fading red, original Texaco sign; an old wooden archway; a cobblestone sidewalk; an iron church bell; a Texas flag; and then the few staff members, who were wearing their pioneer costumes. Before I ever entered, I realized that Buffalo Gap is an oddly picturesque place.

The next fort along the trail was Chadbourne, so we continued on 277 south over steep hills that several times offered and then snatched away a quick view of the mountains. We crossed Oak Creek and made our way to the site of Fort Chadbourne in the town of Bronte, "Where Livin's a Pleasure." Set on private ranch property today, the fort is a beautiful, secluded place to pause from the motion and hustle of the road. Buildings still standing include barracks, surgeon's quarters, a fountain house and the ruins of the Butterfield Stage and Mail Station. The stage route started at St. Louis and Memphis and went all the way to San Francisco. It took twenty-five days and cost each passenger $200 for a one-way trip. For the western portion of the trip, beginning in Texas, the stage operators used mules instead of horses, as they were less desirable to the Indians. While I'm sitting in the comfort of a smooth sedan, it's nearly impossible to imagine that long, bumpy stagecoach ride.

A well-known story brings old Fort Chadbourne to life in my mind, although it is not a trail of blood but rather the human competitive spirit that draws us there. A few officers from Fort Chadbourne challenged the Comanches who camped nearby to a horse race, assuming that the Indians' wild-eyed mustang could be no match for the pristine Kentucky thoroughbred prized by the Texas military. Whatever the stakes, the officers paid dearly in pride—the Comanche rider not only won the race but also completed the final fifty yards turned backward, taunting the officer as he rode.

On our way out of Bronte, we drove past the historical marker for the Indian Rock Shelters, which have provided archaeologists with information about the prehistoric inhabitants of Coke County. The ancient natives used rock ledges as shelter, and they carved images into the walls of some of these caves; they left behind tools, shells and animal bones. For thousands of years, Indian tribes dwelled in these counties that now hold the ruins of both their own primitive domiciles and the forts that the Texans built to fend them off. Paradoxically, the Forts Trail links the structures that housed ancient Indians and those that defeated modern tribes. Following the trail, we crossed Kickapoo Creek and the Colorado River, near the South Fork of the Concho River.

In this part of our drive, we tracked a trail of blood created in 1857. In February, a company from the Second Cavalry originating at Camp Verde in present Kerr County (just two counties south of Fort McKavett) met Comanche raiders in a battle at Kickapoo Creek. They pursued these Indians for miles, and eventually the skirmish ended with two dead on each side. The soldiers made their way to Fort McKavett in the middle of the night, where one wounded, John Martin, died shortly after their arrival.

The military located the site for Fort Concho in 1867, at the point where the Middle Concho and North Concho Rivers converge. They needed a post to replace Fort Chadbourne, which did not have an adequate supply of water. There were a few companies of black troops stationed at Fort Concho, who made great progress in mapping new routes and tracking Indians. One such company set out under the command of Captain Nicholas Nolan to apprehend raiding Indians and retrieve stolen livestock, but the troops experienced extreme suffering as a result. *Along the Texas Forts Trail* gives a description of the famous Nolan Expedition of 1877, which originated at Fort Concho in July of that year:

> *One of the most tragic events in Fort Concho's history occurred in the summer of 1877. On August 3, two black troopers rode into Fort Concho to report that Captain Nicholas Nolan and a detachment of black troopers, Company A, Tenth Cavalry, along with a volunteer company of buffalo hunters were lost on the plains and starving for water. Poor judgment, bad management, and indecision by the leaders resulted in the force being scattered in the desert. Some members of the group made it to water in a matter of hours, but one party of soldiers wandered for days, surviving on only the coagulated blood and heavy urine of dying horses. The majority of the expedition's members survived, but four troopers and one civilian perished, along with twenty-three horses and four mules.*

To be exact, Nolan's men had gone for eighty-six hours without water when they finally reached Double Lakes in Lynn County, just south of Lubbock. The Tenth Cavalry, headquartered at Fort Concho, once again proved their stamina and courageous nature when they defeated Apache chieftain Victorio and essentially rendered the Texas frontier once again safe.

While we were in San Angelo, we attended Christmas at Fort Concho, an annual event that takes place on the grounds of the fort, but it really encompasses the whole town. San Angelo has a quaint little downtown area speckled with antique shops and inviting cafés. We drove through the town square and circled it twice to get a better look. The folks here, like those in Breckenridge, wore their festive sweaters, socks and hats, decorating the busy street corners with their array of red, white and green.

At Fort Concho, the cold December weather did not keep the curious visitors from attending Christmas. Most were families with children, and we walked through tent after tent of merchandise from the frontier period. There were costumes like the gray and blue jackets and knee-length pants that the men wore, swords and turquoise- or ivory-handled pocketknives. There were sheathed daggers and arrows with fur-lined quivers.

There was loose tobacco and pipes, and coins and medallions gleamed from within glass cases. Outside in the center of the fort was a large field where men in the old military uniforms of the 1850s fired cannons and shot muskets. Ladies rode sidesaddle through the grounds, donning the dignified air of those who first lived in these Texas towns and who first patronized the shops and first swept the floors of the houses along the rivers.

We walked through the soldiers' barracks building, which had at least two dozen wooden cots with thin feather mattresses about the thickness of a warm sleeping bag. I could picture the primitive means by which these men lived as I walked across the dirt floor and past the small coal furnace in the center of the room. I remember thinking that I would hope to be one of the two lucky soldiers whose beds were right next to the heater, because those beds all the way at either end surely felt no heat. There was, however, an unlabeled bottle of a copper liquid that appeared to be whiskey lying on a small table between two beds. So that's how they kept warm.

We walked past a round pen where children mingled with sheep and goats and romped with donkeys. The soldiers set down their muskets—leaning them each against the others, bayonets crossed at the top and forming a tall metal teepee with a sharp, shining point at the top. Here in their annual reenactments, the people of San Angelo wander back to the time when

Fort Concho Christmas.

messengers came thundering in on their horses to report that Nolan's men may die of thirst. Here the Butterfield Stage came through bearing weary riders to California in hopes of a fortune in gold. And here white settlers believed that they could safely move into the region, inching the Comanches farther westward with each passing year.

On Sunday morning, the Forts Trail conveyed us to Christoval, Texas. We stopped for breakfast at the Country Junction, where pickups filled the parking lot to its capacity, obstructing our view of the restaurant from the street. I ate spicy sausage patties and eggs over easy while my eyes perused the walls filled with stuffed trophies of all shapes and dimensions. These were the spoils of no archer. The head of a soft-eyed deer was mounted on the wall, as well as game fowl with wings extended. Most of the patrons wore camouflage, and they ate with either the anticipation of the hunt that would follow or the hunger after the one preceding. To create some variety in the decor, the owners of the Country Junction have placed clever silhouettes of western scenes like cowboys leaning on a fence, a horse rearing back on its hind legs or a ranch dog sitting patiently next to his companion. These solid black renderings are the work of an animator who's handy with a scroll saw. As I walked out the door, I noticed three or four tiny plastic stands, each cradling the business card of a local taxidermist.

We crossed Bois D'Arc Draw along the way to El Dorado. Another name for the Osage Orange, the Bois D'Arc's wood is flexible and smooth, making it the perfect material for a handcrafted bow. The Caddo Indians made these bows, as they found the wood in abundance in east Texas, and they found that they could trade them with Indians from other regions. The Bois D'Arc hedges were thorny, and when there came to be inadequate fencing supplies for ranchers, they discovered that they could use nature as a makeshift fence. The Bois D'Arc was considered to be "pig tight, horse high, and bull strong." These thick, thorny branches were the predecessors to the barbed wire fences that came soon after.

Passing through El Dorado on Highway 190, we came eventually to Fort McKavett via Farm Road 864. When such facilities are available at these forts, we usually take a little time to walk through the museum and gift shop of each. McKavett's was my favorite. There were large partitions set up through a circular corridor that related a succinct chronology of the Indian wars in paragraphs and pictures. McKavett's grounds have some ruins, a rebuilt hospital and officers' quarters, but at one time it held a vast collection of permanent buildings, including two-story officers' quarters, a bakery, a laundry facility, enlisted men's barracks, a powder magazine and a hospital. Apparently, I am not alone in my opinion of this one; General Sherman executed a famous inspection tour in 1871 and named McKavett "the prettiest post in Texas."

At one time, Fort McKavett was the operating base for four regiments of black soldiers, and in a real-life enactment of *To Kill a Mockingbird*, a local white farmer shot a black soldier and ultimately escaped punishment. John "Humpy" Jackson discovered a letter that his daughter had received from an enamored black trooper. In his rage, he killed a black soldier, though not the one with whom his daughter had corresponded. According to legend, the military searched two years for Jackson before he surrendered, and he was found innocent of all charges in 1871 when he went to trial.

I was reluctant to leave the "prettiest post," but the Forts Trail beckoned. We stayed on 190 to Menard, Texas, where we picked up Highway 29 into Mason. Before the town itself existed, an unfortunate resident of the Menard vicinity was captured when Kiowa chief Satanta executed a raid throughout the plains in 1864, what would become one of the bloodiest years in the tale of the Texas frontier. Dorothy Field became their captive, and they traveled with her all the way north to Kansas. There is no record of her rescue, but there is evidence that Rangers were still searching for her ten years later.

Driving toward Menard, the archer's blood trail led us back one hundred years before the time of the frontier forts to a time that was equally treacherous—when the Spanish occupied parts of Texas, some for exploration and some for religious crusade. When these proud, ambitious men arrived with horses and artillery into a brand-new world, they encountered tribes of Indians who were at war with one another. In a bitter twist of fate, these weapons and horses that equipped the Spanish when they arrived fell into the grip of the Comanches, and ultimately these warriors surpassed the Spaniards in their skills on horseback and defeated them.

Believing that to embrace the Lipan Apaches and teach them Christian doctrine would be to establish peace with the Indians, the Spanish built the San Saba Mission in 1757. They chose a site bordered on one side by the San Saba River and by the Arroyo de Juan Lorenzo (now Celery Creek) on the other. The Spanish thought that this location would provide an unending supply of water while it protected them from hostile attacks. Unfortunately, they were gravely mistaken. The creek's steep banks allowed the warriors to pass undetected into the boundaries of the mission, and the Presidio built to protect it sat a full half-mile from the mission itself. Colonel Diego Ortiz Parilla, who commanded the Spanish army in that area, raised objections about the vulnerable positioning of the buildings, but they did not heed his warnings.

The Spaniards' relationship with the Apaches caused enmity like they had never seen before. The Comanches and several other plains tribes attacked the San Saba Mission to find the Apaches who might reside there and left nothing but a trail of fire and blood for those few survivors who had befriended their ancient enemies. One of these survivors, Friar Miguel Molina, recorded a detailed personal account of the events of that fateful day. Because we have access to what his eyes and ears perceived, I can imagine what transpired:

Thereupon the Father President went out into the courtyard. I accompanied him, filled with amazement and fear when I saw nothing but Indians on every hand, armed with guns and arrayed in the most horrible attire. Besides the paint on their faces, red and black, they adorned with the pelts and tails of wild beasts, wrapped around them or hanging down from their heads, as well as deer horns. Some were disguised as various kinds of animals, and some wore feather headdresses. All were armed with muskets, swords, and lances (or pikes, as they are generally called), and I noticed also that they had brought with them some youths armed with bows and arrows, doubtless to train and encourage them in their cruel and bloody way of life.

As soon as the wily enemy became aware of the confidence we placed in them, many dismounted and, without waiting for us to unlock the gates, opened them by wrenching off the crossbars with their hands. This done, they crowded into the inner stockade, as many of them as it would hold, about three hundred, a few more or less. They resorted to the stratagem of extending their arms toward our people and making gestures of civility and friendliness. When I noticed that many chieftains had approached with similar gestures, I advised and persuaded the Father President to order that they be given bundles of tobacco and other things they prize highly. This he did most generously. I myself presented four bundles to an Indian who never did dismount and whom the others acknowledged as their Great Chief. He was a Comanche, according to the barbarians themselves, and worthy of respect. His war dress and his red jacket were well decorated, after the manner of French uniforms, and he was fully armed. His face was hideous and extremely grave.

When I gave him the four bundles of tobacco, he accepted them cautiously, but with a contemptuous laugh, and gave no other sign of acknowledgment. I was disconcerted at this, all the more so because I had already seen that the Indians, heedless of their promises of peace, were stealing the kettles and utensils from the kitchen, and the capes of the soldiers. They also took the horses from the corral, and then demanded more. When they were told there were no more, they asked whether there were many horses at the Presidio. The Fathers and soldiers told them that there were indeed many horses at the Presidio, as well as equipment and supplies of all kinds -a reply we thought expedient to make them fully aware that nothing was lacking for the defense of the Presidio. When we asked the cunning enemy whether they intended to visit the Commandant at the Presidio, they replied that they did, and asked us to give them a note to him. We did not consider his request inopportune, but rather thought it might be an effective way of clearing the mission of the enemy, for they still had it completely surrounded and were causing great damage by their thievery, as they boldly ransacked all the buildings and offices.

Desiring retaliation for the sack of the Presidio, Colonel Parilla escorted 360 Spanish soldiers and 176 Indians north toward the Red River. After fighting the Comanches and their allies for four hours, Parilla and his men had to retreat, leaving their cannons and several weapons behind. The Comanches proved their resilience and imperviousness in the events surrounding the attack on the San Saba Mission. Like a child's quest for the place where a rainbow meets the earth, conquering the Comanche and submitting them to the Spaniards' laws and religion was a lofty and fruitless endeavor. It would require another one hundred years and an opponent with much more ardor and resolve to wrest the plains from their desperate grip.

We followed where the history led. Highway 29 east to Mason, Texas, through cactus-speckled mountains along the way. On the roadside, a historic marker describes Pegleg Crossing, a favorite mountain pass of Indians as well as "adventurers, mustang hunters, Indian fighters, German settlers, gold-seekers." It became a stage station that was notorious for holdups. The Spanish fought Apaches here in the 1730s before they attempted peace via the construction of the mission. We entered Mason on a Sunday's mid-afternoon, and like a magnet pulling another into its field, Santos Taqueria drew Rick's Cadillac through the town square and into its last available parking space.

It is worth mentioning here that a secondary goal—or even tertiary and beyond, for what we have now come to learn classifies us as Heritage Tourists—has evolved in the mere practice of our embarking on these road trips and also in our necessity for sustenance that is both repeated daily and unrelenting. The goal has become, of course, to find the best and most authentic Mexican food. While it takes quite the back seat to the enterprise of finding and revealing the places where blood was shed for possession of the land where we can now safely and freely roam, this is no small task, and it is not to be taken lightly. There is, I have found, some correlation between the caliber of the food and the decor of the place in question. In the places where the food is unquestionably authentic, the common denominator appears to be an exuberant prominence of the color red. It might anger the bulls down there, but in these parts the plastic red roses, red velvet curtains, carpet and cloth napkins and the paintings depicting the red ruffled tiers of the ladies' skirts are a sure sign of great food ahead. Another way to determine whether a place will make the list is if part or all of the menu is written in Spanish. In these cases, you can order by number, and no. 1 all the way to no. 43 is certain to be a hit. One note: those more adventurous or more carnivorous may want to try the *Tacos con Lengua*, but I usually stick with *pollo*.

When I walked into Santos and looked around, I immediately subjected it to the criteria formed by our past experiences, and I was a little unsure. The restaurant was minimally decorated in earth tones, with several pieces of southwestern-style pottery. The menu—printed on a giant sign on the wall over the heads of two long-haired young men who served as both cook and cashier—looked like the menu in a college campus sandwich shop. We ordered at the counter and grabbed a table after pouring some of the homemade salsa out of a pitcher into paper cups. While we waited for the food, I noticed T-shirts and sweatshirts for sale, bearing the Santos Taqueria logo and costing about twenty dollars apiece. It turned out that the food was unbelievably excellent, and we were both shocked to have our expectations so remarkably surpassed. Santos made the list, and Mason, Texas, became for me a place worth a longer look.

We drove outside of town up a steep hill, where a reproduction of Fort Mason's barracks now stands. It was originally built in 1851 and strategically positioned on Post Hill, providing an incomparable vantage point. In written descriptions of the fort, nearly all its visitors commented on the view from the top of the hill. I, too, wouldn't mind being the owner of that land—the fort's one remaining building sits proudly above the rest of the town, and a Texas flag waves farewell to those descending and beckons those approaching. Robert E. Lee commanded troops who were stationed here before his more famous role in the Civil War. Fort Mason also served as a prison camp for Union sympathizers for a short time. However, Santos Taqueria and the climb to the top of Post Hill are only two of the treasures tucked neatly inside Mason, Texas. It is also the only location in the Lone Star state where topaz exists, buried deep in the soil in ravines and creek beds. Two ranches in Mason County allow people to dig for Texas's state stone for a reasonable fee. You can camp at night and become a hunter by day, sifting dirt through mesh screens for the rocks that gleam rich gold or pale blue.

Fed and having stretched our legs, we followed the Forts Trail along Highway 386 north and then 71 west to Brady, called the Heart of Texas for its location at the geographical center of the state. It's hard to miss evidence of Brady residents' pride in this claim to fame as you pass such places as the Heart of Texas Bed & Breakfast and the Country Music Museum. There is the cleverly named Hard 8 Barbecue Restaurant, depicting a pair of dice, each showing a four, and an eight-point buck. The trail weaves through town and comes out on Highway 190 eastbound.

Along 190, we passed two historical markers within half a mile of each other. The first describes the Historic Soldiers' Water Hole, where Robert E. Lee led his troops to water when they were in the vicinity scouting for marauding Indians. Immigrants camped nearby as well, using this location to revive their tired, thirsty families while they made the difficult trek westward. Twenty-seven Indians attacked one such group of eighteen men, women and children in 1850. They murdered the families and stole their horses. A little farther lies the site for the 1866 Onion Creek Indian Fight, where the whites retrieved stolen horses from an Indian camp. An arrow struck one of these men in the head, and certainly against all medical odds, they removed the arrowhead with a pocketknife and he survived the injury. What a larger-than-life story he must have told his grandchildren!

We continued along the Forts Trail, turning north onto Highway 45 at the town of Richland Springs. There were bloody incidents around this town in the 1850s, and a few witnesses lived to pass the stories on. Our drive from Brady to Richland Springs traces the path that a posse from Richland Creek took when it pursued a band of Indians who murdered Beardy Hall. In eye-for-an-eye fashion, the members of the posse killed one Indian and gave his scalp to Hall's son, Alex, who displayed it on a fence post for quite awhile.

In Richland Springs, there was an unofficial fort privately owned and located on the Duncan brothers' ranch. There, families "forted up" when threats of Indians were imminent. In 1858, a company of rangers camped near the location of the old Fort Duncan, and they sent two men out to scout a path through which to take their wagons. Indians attacked, and the men ran back to camp. To the great consternation of the Indians, I'm sure, the ranger company outnumbered them, so a running fight ensued, and the rangers killed four and recovered several stolen horses.

Like a vicious game of volleyball, back and forth the depredations went—one, two, even three in a row for the Indians, and then a few lives and horses taken back by the whites. In blood and tears they fill their scorecards until, eventually and inevitably, someone gets the victory. The frontier forts are all connected on this drive by the highways that lead to them and the towns that developed because of them. But having seen the ruins and heard the muskets fired at Fort Concho's Christmas and having passed the forks and creeks where individuals ripped arrowheads from underneath their skin, it is more realistic for me to visualize the route as a crimson trail of blood. It only requires a look backward in time, a reliable sedan, an archer's stance with feet planted wide, a tight elbow and a steady pull of the bow.

Road Trip Maps and Directions

The following pages contain the maps that serve as companions to our road trip narratives. These maps include the locations of roadside historical markers, forts and places of interest along the lesser-traveled Texas highways.

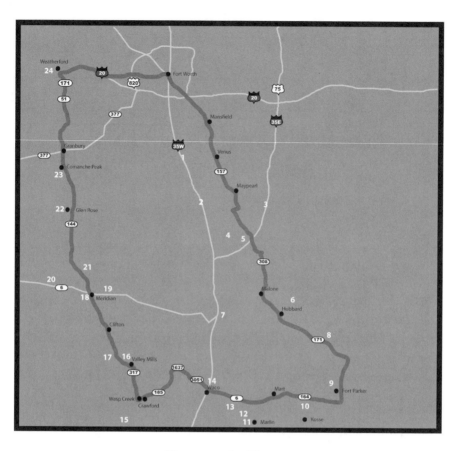

PARKER'S FORT

1	Norman Springs	6921 U.S. 67 at I-35, Alvarado
2	Grandview Cemetery	FM 4, just E of CR 401, Grandview
3	Chambers' Creek	Forreston, take U.S. 77 S 1 mi.
4	Ft. Smith	Itasca, take FM 934 8 mi. E to FM 4319
5	James McDaniel	E. Water St. off U.S. 77, Milford
6	Battle Creek Burial Ground	From Dawson, go W on SH 31 about 2 mi.
7	Old Carr Ranch	1 mi. S of Abbott on Willie Nelson Rd.
8	Tehuacana Cemetery	CR 226 at Westminster St., Tehuacana
9	Ft. Parker	From Mexia, SR 14 about 9 mi. to Park Rd. 35
10	William F. Williams	Kosse, SH 14 2 mi. S; on east side of road
11	Capt. Henry Gray Carter	407 Gift St., Marlin

12	Indian Battlefield	SH 6 N of Marlin about 6.5 mi.
12	Falls of the Brazos River	FM 712 SW 5 mi. to east bank of Brazos River
12	Ft. Milam	FM 712 4 mi. SW; FM 2027 S 2 mi.
13	Mustang Prairie	SH 7 16 mi. E of Marlin; SW SH 14 3 mi. to CR 283
14	Waco Indian Village	Waco Dr. behind Taylor Museum of Waco History
14	Ft. Fisher/TX Ranger Museum	University Parks Avenue and I-35N, Waco
14	Rangers/Fence-Cutting Wars	Entrance to Ft. Fisher
15	Ft. Gates	SH 36, Ft. Gates St., Gatesville
16	Bosque River Crossing	China Spring, 2 mi. W; Baylor Camp Rd. S to FM 1637
17	Roden Taylor Crain	Valley Mills Cemetery, NW of Valley Mills off SH 6
17	Odle Log Cabin	Valley Mills, FM217 W; CR3155 W; Odle Ln. North; CR401
18	Bosque County	SH 22 0.7 mi. W of Meridian
19	John A. Lomax home	SH 144 N of Meridian 1 mi. to picnic area
20	William Berry Smith	Iredell, FM 1238 4 mi. S 1.5 mi. past Marker Ranch
21	"Buck" Barry and J.J. Cureton	Walnut Springs Park, south side of town on SH 144
22	Barnard's Trading Post #2	U.S. 67, 8 mi. E of Glen Rose
22	Barnard's Mill	315 Barnard St., Glen Rose
22	Squaw Creek Indian Fight	Hwy. 67 E of Glen Rose 0.9 mi., FM 144 N 1.8 mi.
23	Comanche Peak	From Granbury, take SH 144 about 3 mi. S
24	Porter Cemetery	Take U.S. 180 about 10 mi. W of Weatherford
24	Bose Ikard's Grave	Greenwood Cemetery, Front St.
24	Oliver Loving's Grave	Greenwood Cemetery, Front St.
24	Double Log Cabin	Holland Lake Park, Santa Fe Drive

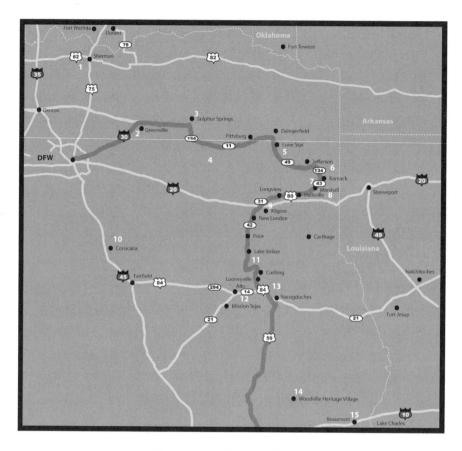

FOREST TRAIL EAST

1	Colbert's Ferry	U.S. 75, 5 mi. N, Denison
1	Sand Springs	U.S. 75, corner of Loy Lake and Park Lane
1	Dwight Eisenhower birthplace	Lamar Avenue and Day St.
1	First site of Sherman	U.S. 82, 4 mi. W; Preston Rd. N 0.5 mi. to Cherokee Trail
1	Butterfield Overland Mail	Courthouse lawn, Lamar and Travis (SH 56), Sherman
1	Ft. Inglish	Near corner of Lipscomb and 9th St., Bonham
1	Ft. Lyday	FM 904, 8 mi. NE of Ladonia
2	Greenville	2821 Washington St., at Municipal Building
2	Headwaters of Sabine River	U.S. 69, 1.3 mi. NW of Celeste
2	King's Fort	607 N Clay St. Kaufman
3	Early Sulphur Bluff	FM 71, 0.5 mi. E on SW corner of Bluff Cemetery

3	Battle of the Neches	Roadside park on Hwy. 20, 5 mi. E of Colfax
4	Indian cemetery and village	SH 37 5 mi. NE of Quitman to CR 1416
5	Old Spearman's Ferry	U.S. 259, 1 mi. S of Lone Star in Morris County
6	Potter's Point	Hwy. 49 at FM 727, 4 mi. E of Smithland
7	Marshall Shreveport Stage	SH 43 at Pine Bluff Rd., 5.5 mi. NE of Marshall
8	Sam Houston	128 E. Columbia (SH 21/147)
9	World's Richest Acre	Main and Commerce Sts., Kilgore
10	Corsicana oil field discovery	400 Block of 12th Street
11	Cook's Fort	About 3 mi. S of Rusk on FM 241
11	McLean-Sheridan Massacres	8 mi. S of Palestine via FM 2419 to E CR
12	Homer-Alto Rd.	U.S. 69 and FM 1911, 10.5 mi. S of Alto
12	Box's Fort	9 mi. W of Alto on SH 294
12	Lacy's Fort	About 2.5 mi. W of Alto on SH 21
12	Town of Mt. Sterling	FM 225 7 mi. S of Douglass
12	Mission Concepcion	FM 225 7 mi. S of Douglass; S on CR 789
12	Presidio Dolores	FM 225, 14 mi. W and 6 mi. S of Douglass at CR 789
12	Sam Houston/San Augustine	SH 21/147 (128 E. Columbia)
12	Battle of Fredonia	SH 21, 0.4 mi. E of Carrizo Creek
13	Mission Guadalupe	North and Mullen St., Nacogdoches
13	Battle of Nacogdoches	Corner of Fredonia and El Camino Real (Main)
13	Thompson family	SH 21, 7 mi. E, Chapel Creek Cemetery
14	San Augustine	U.S. 96 and SH 21
14	Confederate Refugees in Texas	SH 19/154, 0.5 mi. N of San Augustine, roadside park
14	Mission Dolores de los Ais	FM 147, 0.5 mi. S of San Augustine
15	Lucas Gusher/Spindletop	3 mi. S of Beaumont on Spindletop Avenue
15	Richard Dowling	SH 73, 15 mi. SW, Port Arthur

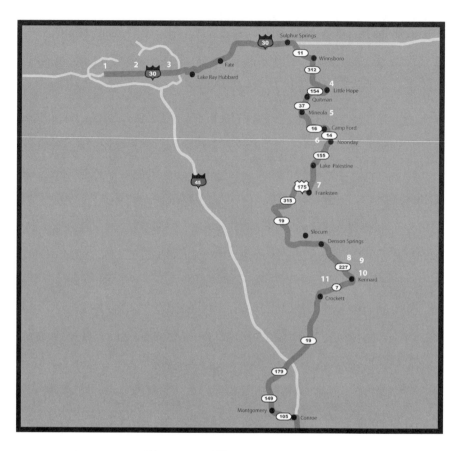

FOREST TRAIL WEST

1	Allen Log Cabin	White Settlement Historical Museum, 8320 Hanon Dr.
1	Eastern Cattle Trail	Heritage Park, 100 N. Commerce, Ft. Worth
1	"Where the West Begins"	NW corner Houston and W. Belknap, Ft. Worth
1	Livestock Exchange	201 E. Exchange St., Ft. Worth
1	TX Log Cabins and Museum	University and Colonial Parkway, Ft. Worth
1	Hell's Half Acre	12th and Houston, Ft. Worth
1	Quanah Parker	131 E. Exchange St., Ft. Worth
1	Stockyards	100 Block of E. Exchange St., Ft. Worth
2	Sloan-Journey Expedition	Mosier Valley Rd. and FM 157, Arlington
2	Bird's Fort	FM 157, 1 mi. N of Trinity River, Arlington
2	Village Creek	Lakewood Dr., Arlington Golf Course, 7th tee

2	Mid Cities: Grapevine Springs	700 S. Park Rd., Grapevine Springs Park, Coppell
2	Peters Colony	FM 1171, W. City Park, Lewisville
2	Marrow Bone Spring	Founders Park, Matlock and Arkansas, Arlington
2	Johnson Station Cemetery	1100 Block, W. Mayfield and S. Cooper (FM 157)
2	Chisholm Cattle Trail	SH 360 east side near SH 183, Arlington
2	General Edward Tarrant	Spur 303, Arlington, 0.1 mi. W of Green Oaks
2	Top O'Hill Terrace	3001 U.S. 80 (W. Division), Arlington
2	Goodwin Log Cabin	1400 Block of S. Carrier Pkwy., Grand Prairie
2	Cross Timbers	2602 Mayfield Rd., Grand Prairie
2	Cherokees in Dallas	Old City Park at 1717 Gano St., Dallas
3	General R.M. Gano (CSA)	S. Oakland St. (main road, left at circle) Dallas
3	Dallas County	Dallas County Historical Plaza (Elm, Market and Main)
3	John Neely Bryan	Dealey Plaza, Elm and Houston, Dallas
3	Sam Bass train robbery	200 Block of W. Main near flagpole, Mesquite
4	Indian cemetery and villages	5 mi. NE of Quitman on SH 37 to CR 1416
5	Mineola	On SR 37, TX Main St. City, founded in 1873
6	Cherokee chief Bowles	From Canton, SH 64 19 mi. SE to CR 4923, 2.5 mi.
7	Ft. Houston	U.S. 79 and FM 1990, 2 mi. S of Palestine
7	McLean Massacre	8 mi. S of Palestine via FM 2419 to E CR
7	Kickapoo Battlefield	2 mi. SE of Frankston on FM 19; just before CR
8	Edens-Madden Massacre	FM 227 10 mi. E of Grapeland
9	Mission Tejas	Grapeland, SH 21 N 1.5 mi., Park Road 44 0.5 mi.
10	Elisha Clapp	SH 21 10 mi. N of Crockett; FM 2967 N 2.5 mi.
11	Daniel McLean Claim	1.5 mi. W of Weches on SH 21

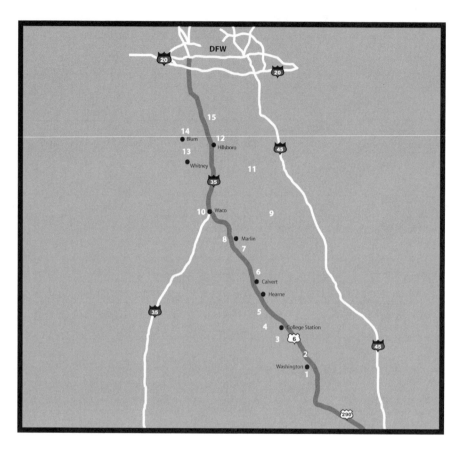

Highway 6 Trail

1	Washington	Washington-on-the-Brazos State Park
1	Star of the Republic Museum	23200 Park Rd. 12, Washington
2	Primus Kelly	SH 6 S from Navasota 12 mi. to roadside park
2	Rene Robert LaSalle	SH 90, 400 Block E. Washington, west end of Esplanade
3	Texas A&M University	SH 6 (business) off Texas Ave. at main A&M campus entrance
3	The Falls of the Brazos River	FM 60, 6 mi. W of College Station
3	Ft. Oldham	Bryan, SH 21 E 20 mi. to Cook's Point
4	Ft. Tenoxtitlan	Caldwell, SH 21 E 5 mi. to roadside park on south side
4	Millican, CSA	FM 2154 at FM 159, 16 mi. S of College Station
5	Ft. Sullivan	Hearne, CR 259 1 mi. off FM 485/CR 260, 1.3 mi.

5	Camp Millican	FM 2154 3 mi. NW of Millican; 1 mi. W on High Prairie
6	Harvey Massacre	SH 6, 5 mi. N of Calvert
7	Indian Battlefield	From Marlin, take SH 6 N about 6.5 mi.
8	Ft. Milam	FM 712 4 mi. SW; FM 2027 S 2 mi. local road E 0.7 mi.
9	Ft. Parker	From Mexia, Hwy. 14 to Park Rd. 35
10	Ft. Fisher/TX Rangers Museum	University Parks Ave. and I-35N, Waco
11	Battle Creek Burial Ground	From Dawson, go W on SH 31 about 2 mi.
12	Hillsboro	118 S. Waco St., Hillsboro
13	Ft. Graham	5.3 mi. FM 933 N of Whitney; W on FM 2604 to park
14	Philip Nolan	From Blum, take SH 174 N about 3 mi. to marker
15	Ft. Smith	FM 934 and FM 4319, 8 mi. E of Itasca, across road

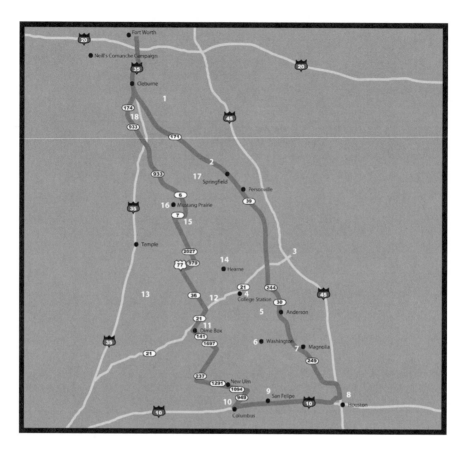

Early Settlements

1	Battle Creek Burial Ground	From Dawson, go W on SH 31 about 2 mi.
2	Ft. Boggy	From Centerville, I-45 S about 5 mi. to rest area
3	Old San Antonio Road	SW corner Hwy. 410 and Nacogdoches in parking lot
4	Ft. Tenoxtitlan	From Caldwell, SH 21 E 5 mi. to roadside park on south side
4	Brazos River	FM 60, 6 mi. W of College Station
4	Ft. Oldham	From Bryan, SH 21 E 20 mi. to Cook's Point
4	Texas A&M University	SH 6 (business) off TX Ave. at main A&M campus entrance
5	Chappell Hill	U.S. 290 at FM 1155
5	Lockhart Plantation	Old U.S. 290, 1 mi. E
5	Primus Kelly	SH 6 S from Navasota 12 mi. to roadside park

5	La Bahia Trail	La Salle (Business SH 6) and Bruce St., Cedar Creek Park
6	Washington on the Brazos	Washington-on-the-Brazos State Park
6	Star of the Republic Museum	- 23200 Park Rd. 12, Washington
7	Magnolia	11 mi. SW, at SW corner of SH 294 and FM 1990
8	Camp on San Jacinto	Off the Houston Ship Channel in LaPorte
9	Early Roads to San Felipe	S.F. Austin State Park, PR 38 (off FM 1458), San Felipe
10	Rangers of Austin Colony	Spring and Bowie Sts., Columbus
11	Dime Box	FM 141 at Slayton Ave., NW side
11	Dime Box Museum	Dime Box Heritage Museum, 1103 FM 141
11	Old Dime Box	Dime SH 21, 5 mi. NW
12	Ft. Oldham	2.5 mi. SW of Cooks Point, near FM 1362 and CR 226
13	Mission San Ildefonso	About 5 mi. from present-day Rockdale in Milam County
14	Ft. Sullivan	CR 259 1 mi. off FM 485/CR 260, about 1.3 mi.
15	Falls on the Brazos	FM 712 SW 5 mi. to east bank of Brazos River in park
15	Ft. Milam	From Marlin, FM 712 4 mi. SW; FM 2027 S 2 mi.
15	Indian battlefield	From Marlin, SH 6 N 6.5 mi.
16	Mustang Prairie	SH 7 16 mi. E of Marlin; 3 mi. SW on SH 14 to CR 283
17	Springfield	SH 14, 500 ft. south of Ft. Parker State Park entrance
18	Ft. Graham	5.3 mi. FM 933 N of Whitney; W on FM 2604 to park

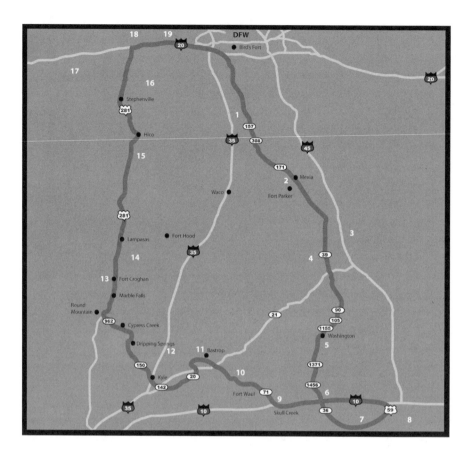

THE TEXAS INDEPENDENCE TRAIL

1	Ft. Smith	FM 934 and FM 4319, 8 mi. E of Itasca, across road
2	Battle Creek Engagement	2 mi. W of Dawson on SH 31
2	Battle Creek Burial Ground	From Dawson, W on SH 31 about 2 mi.
2	Ft. Parker	From Mexia, SR 14 about 9 mi. to Park Rd. 35
3	Ft. Boggy	From Centerville, I-45 S 5 mi. southbound, rest area
4	Dunn's Fort	SW of Wheelock, near Robertson-Brazos border
5	Chappell Hill	U.S. 290 at FM 1155
5	Lockhart Plantation	Old U.S. 290, 1 mi. E
6	Bellville	30 S. Holland St. off SH 36
6	Austin Colony	SH 36/159 0.5 mi. NW of Bellville
6	Primus Kelly	SH 6, 11 mi. S of Navasota in roadside park

7	Ft. Bend Museum	500 Houston St., Richmond
7	George Ranch Historic Park	10215 FM Rd. 762, Richmond
7	Jane Long Boardinghouse	200 Block N. 4th between Morton and Calhoun, Richmond
8	Sam Houston Heritage Park	400 Block of McKinney, Houston
8	Old Harrisburg	8100 Block of Lawndale at Frio Frost Bank
8	Camp on the San Jacinto	Off the Houston Ship Channel in LaPorte
9	Rangers of Austin Colony	Spring and Bowie Sts., Columbus
10	Ft. Waul	0.25 mi. N of U.S. 183 and 90A, Gonzales
11	Gotier Trace (Bastrop)	Bastrop State Park, Loop 150 and SH 21
12	Camp Mabry	Camp Mabry ground, near W 35th St. entry, Austin
12	Texas State History Museum	800 N. Congress Ave., Austin
13	Ft. Croghan	Ft. Croghan Museum grounds, 703 SH 29 W, Burnet
14	Black's Fort	From Bertram, FM 1174 N 8 mi.; E on CR 210A 2 mi.
15	Miss Ann Whitney	U.S. 281 N 7-8 blocks from Hamilton Courthouse Sq.
16	Comanche Peak	From Granbury, take SH 144 about 3 mi. S
17	Desdemona	Ft. Blair, CSA; SH 16 at S. Desdemona city limits
18	Oliver Loving home, 1855	U.S. 281 N of Mineral Wells 7.5 mi.; Loving Rd. W 0.25 mi.
19	Porter Cemetery	Take U.S. 180 about 10 mi. W of Weatherford
19	Bose Ikard's Grave	Greenwood Cemetery, Front St.
19	Oliver Loving's Grave	Greenwood Cemetery, Front St.
19	Double Log Cabin	Holland Lake Park, Santa Fe Drive

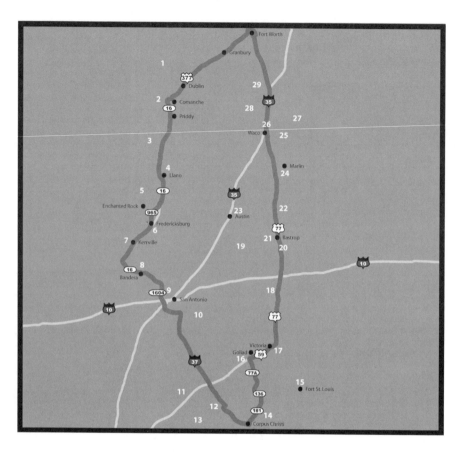

HILL COUNTRY/BUFFALO HUMP'S RAID

1	Ft. Blair, CSA	SH 16 at south city limits, Desdemona
2	Indian Raid in Comanche	Courthouse Square, Comanche
3	Comanche Indian Treaty	FM 2732 off U.S. 190, SW of San Saba
3	Camp San Saba	FM 1955, 10 mi. S of Brady, off U.S. 87
4	Baby Head Cemetery	From Llano, take SH 16 N approx. 9 mi. to ROW
5	Old Fort Mason	Junction of U.S. 87 and U.S. 377 1 mi. N of Mason
6	Ft. Martin Scott	Take U.S. 290 E 2 mi. to ROW, Fredricksburg
7	Cypress Creek Indian sites	FM 1341, 10 mi. E of Kerrville
7	Dowdy Tragedy of 1878	SH 27, 17 mi. NW of Kerrville
8	Battle of Bandera Pass	FM 689 N 10 mi. to Hwy. 16; on 173 ROW
8	Old Texas Ranger Trail	Main and Pecan, facing courthouse, Bandera

9	Ft. Sam Houston Museum	1207 Stanley Rd., San Antonio
9	The Alamo	Alamo Plaza, San Antonio
9	Mission San Juan Capistrano	Mission/Espada Rd., S of Loop 13, San Antonio
10	Mission de las Cabras	From Floresville, take SH 97 2 mi. S to marker
11	Stringfield Massacre	From Tilden, Hwy. 16 23 mi. to 624; W 2.5 mi.
12	Ft. Casa Blanca, CSA	SH 359 at CR 264, Sandia
13	Battle of Agua Dulce	SH 44, east side of Agua Dulce
14	Camp San Fernando	From Kingsville, U.S. 77 (business) 3 mi. N
14	Hynes Bay (Karankawa)	E of Ocean Drive and S. Alameda, Corpus Christi
14	Ft. Lipantitlan	FM 3088 20.1 mi. NW of Corpus Christi; 12 mi. NW of FM 70
15	Ft. St. Louis	SW corner of FM 444 and U.S. 59, Inez
16	Goliad Massacre	From Fannin, 1 mi. S on 2508 from U.S. 59, to park
16	Mission Espiritu de Zuniga	U.S. 183/77A S 1 mi. to park
16	Nuestra Senora del Rosario	U.S. 59 W about 4 mi.
16	Presidio de la Bahia	U.S. 183/77A S 1 mi. to Spur 71
17	Camp Henry E. McCulloch	U.S. 87, 4.1 mi. N of courthouse, Victoria
17	DeWitt's Colony/Kerr's Settlers	FM 146 west side of Kerr Creek, E. Gonzales city limits
18	Old Hanging Tree	West side of U.S. 77, north city limits, Hallettsville
19	Gotier family	Bastrop State Park, Loop 150 and SH 21
19	Wood's Fort	From West Point, State 71 W 1.5 mi. to CR 117
20	The Dawson Expedition/ Historic Oak	Corner of Washington and Colorado, LaGrange
21	Indian Camp Branch	Picnic area on U.S. 77 just south of Lexington
22	Kenny's Fort	U.S. 79, Round Rock
22	Sam Bass death site	W. Main St. at Round Rock Ave.
23	Texas History Museum	800 N. Congress Ave., Austin
24	Ft. Milam	FM 712 SW 4 mi.; 2027 S 2 mi.; local road E 0.7 mi.
25	Indian battlefield	From Marlin, take SH 6 N about 6.5 mi.
26	Ft. Fisher/TX Rangers Museum	University Parks Avenue and I-35N, Waco
27	Battle Creek Burial Ground	From Dawson, go W on SH 31 about 2 mi.
28	Ft. Graham	Whitney to FM 933 N 5.3 mi.; FM 2604 W
29	Ft. Smith	FM 934 8 mi. E of Itasca to FM 4319

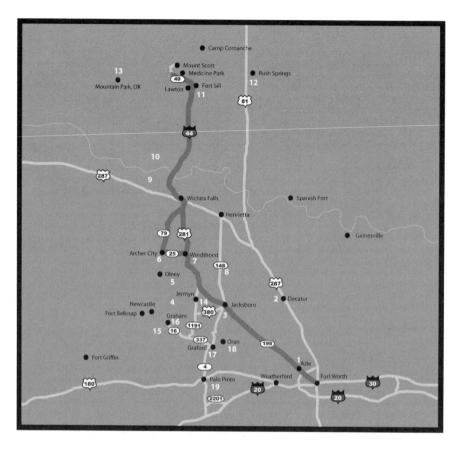

CROSSING THE RED/FORT SILL

1	Kiowa Raid/Walnut Creek	FM 730 ROW E side, 0.75 mi. W of FM 730/SH 199
2	Chisholm Trail	SE corner of Decatur Courthouse Square
2	Jesse and Frank James's campsite	U.S. 380 E of Decatur about 5 mi.
2	TX ranger Captain Ira Long	81/287 S 3 mi.; 4227 S 0.5 mi.; 4226 0.5 mi. W
2	Randolph Vesey	State St., at east side of Courthouse Square
2	Randolph (Uncle Ran) Vesey	Oak Lawn Cem., N. Decatur; by telephone pole
2	Sam Woody's Cabin	U.S. 81/87 3 mi. S to CR 4227; 5 mi. S to cabin
2	Battle of the Knobs	N on FM 730, left on Old Decatur Rd. 2 mi.
2	Indian captives Dot and Bianca Babb	From Chico, FM 1810 about 2 mi. E
3	Ft. Richardson	U.S. 281 0.5 mi. S of Jacksboro
3	Butterfield Stage Line	U.S. 281, N of Lost Creek Bridge

3	Lost Valley	U.S. 281 12 mi. N to roadside park
3	Cavalry Post Hospital, 1867	U.S. 281 S. Ft. Richardson
3	James B. Dosher	Ft. Richardson Interpretive Center
4	Warren Wagon Train	From Graham, take SH 16 about 8 mi. NE
5	Little Salt Creek fight	From Olney, take SH 199 about 6 mi. SE
6	Battle of the Little Wichita	Archer City, FM 25 N 2 mi. to roadside park
6	French Trading	Archer City, FM 25 N 2 mi. to FM 210
6	Camp Cureton, CSA	W of Archer City Courthouse, SH 79 and Center St.
6	Comanche exodus route	SH 114, city park, Megargel
7	Marcy Trail	4.5 mi. S on U.S. 281, Windthorst
7	Battle of Stone Houses	U.S. 281 5 mi. S, then 5 mi. S on Hwy. 16
7	Antelope	SH 281 12 mi. S of Windthorst
8	Buffalo Springs	Junction FM 174 and FM 3077, Buffalo Springs
9	10th Cavalry Creek	Burkburnett (Wichita County) SH 240, 14 mi. W
10	Big Pasture	U.S. 70, in Grandfield, Tillman County
11	Ft. Sill and Museum	I-44, Exit 41, Lawton, OK
11	Mt. Scott	Take SR 49 W off I-44 in Lawton, OK
12	Battle of Wichita Village	U.S. 180, on the north edge of Rush Springs
13	Camp Radziminski	U.S. 183, 1 mi. N of Mountain Park, OK
14	Jermyn community	SH 114, 1 mi. E of Jermyn
14	Loving Ranch House	SH 114 about 3 mi. W, 300 yds. south of site
15	Ft. Belknap and Museum	SH 251, from Newcastle, about 3 mi. S
15	Elm Creek Raid	U.S. 380 W of Newcastle about 8 mi.
16	Brit Johnson	FM 1769, N of Graham
16	Young County Jail	612 Fourth Street, Graham
16	Brazos River Indian Reservation	SH 16 in Graham
16	Wildcatter Ranch	6.5 mi. S of Graham
17	Bevers and Crawford	2 and 3 mi. W of Graford
17	Comanche Trail Through Palo Pinto	1.5 mi. S of SH 16 and FM 337
18	Black Springs	FM 52, Oran
18	Charles Goodnight	FM 52, Oran
19	Old County Jail	1 block S of Courthouse Square, Palo Pinto
19	Jonathan Hamilton Baker	Courthouse Square, Palo Pinto
19	George Webb Slaughter	FM 4, 5 mi. N of Palo Pinto

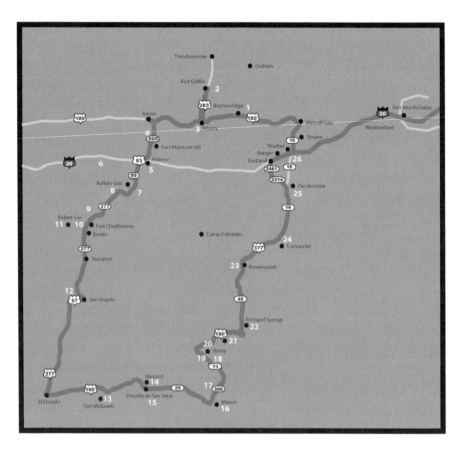

TEXAS FORTS TRAIL

1	Picketville Fort	From Breckenridge, U.S. 183 N about 1 mi. to marker
1	S.P. Newcomb	10.4 mi. NW 183; 1.7 mi. E on FM 1481; 2.5 mi. N on CR 285
2	Ft. Griffin	U.S. 283 N about 15 mi.; Westward Drive into Ft. Griffin Park
3	Ledbetter Picket House	Webb Park, 112 Main Street, Albany
3	Butterfield Mail and Stage	Hwy. 180 9 mi. W of Abilene
4	Ft. Phantom Hill	FM 600 10 mi. N of Abilene
4	Ft. Phantom Hill, CSA	U.S. 277 and 180, County Courthouse, Anson
4	Ft. Phantom Hill Ruins	Take U.S. 180 E about 10 mi. to FM 600 S about 8.5 mi. to ruins
4	Old Ft. Phantom Hill Corn Rd.	From Abilene, SR 351 to 604 SW 5 mi., just inside gate

5	Early Cattle Trail	Corner of S. 1st and Leggett Drive, on T&P Railroad Tow, Abilene
6	Castle Peak	From Merkel, take FM 1235 S about 7 mi.
7	Buffalo Gap Cemetery	From Buffalo Gap, go about 1 mi. W on Hwy. 89 to cemetery
8	Vicinity of Coronado's Camp	From Abilene, take Hwy. 277 SW about 15 mi. to Junction 8
9	Route of the So. Overland	From Bronte, take U.S. 277 N about 11 mi. to roadside park 9
10	Ft. Chadbourne	City hall grounds, 100 Block of S. Washington St., Bronte
11	Fence-Cutting	Courthouse Square, 7th and Austin Ave., Robert Lee
11	General Robert E. Lee	City hall, 7th and Austin Ave.
11	Panther Gap	Robert Lee Cemetery, on SH 158 at east city limits
11	Richard Coke	Courthouse Square 7th and Austin Avenue
12	Ft. Concho	Oakes St. at corner of Oakes and Ave. D, San Angelo
13	Major Ben Ficklin	U.S. 306 access road SW side, where it crosses Ben Ficklin Rd.
13	Ft. McKavett	U.S. 190 for 17 mi. W to FM 864; 6 mi. SW to fort
14	Arroyo de Lorenzo	On U.S. 190 at Celery Creek Bridge, 1.5 mi. W of Menard
14	Mission San Saba	0.5 mi. off U.S. 190, about 1.5 mi. W of Menard
14	Puerto Baluartes	On U.S. 83, 1 mi. S of Menard in roadside park
15	Pegleg Crossing San Saba	On SH 29 ROW, about 10 mi. SE of Menard
16	Ft. Mason and Camp Llano	Mason County Courthouse Square (southeast corner)
16	John Bate Berry	From Mason, take SH 29 about 4 mi. W to Grit Cemetery
16	Old Fort Mason	1 mi. N on U.S. 87 in roadside park at U.S. 87 and U.S. 377
16	Todd Mountain	2.5 mi. S on RR 1723, then 1 mi. SW on RR 2389 right-of-way
17	Chief Katemcy Park	RR 1222 and Katemcy Rd., 11.5 mi. N of Ft. Mason
18	Camp San Saba	FM 1955, in Camp San Saba, 10 mi. S of Brady off U.S. 87

(continued on next page)

19	General Ben McCulloch	SW corner of Courthouse Square, U.S. 337/87 at U.S. 190
20	1870s cowboys and Indians fight	U.S. 87 about 16.2 mi. W to marker, just E of FM 503, Brady
20	Indian battle	U.S. 190 W 10.9 mi. to FM 1311; then S 3.3 mi., Brady
20	Onion Creek Indian fight	U.S. 190 N of Brady about 6 mi.
20	Western Trail	U.S. 283 10 mi. N to marker between "Brady Mountains"
21	Soldier's Waterhole	U.S. 190 E about 5.5 mi.; take CR 412 E 2.5 mi. to marker
22	John Duncan's Fort	On U.S. 190 and Hwy. 45, Richland Springs
23	Camp Collier, CSA	Brown County Courthouse, Broadway and Center
23	Greenleaf Fisk	Courthouse Square, Center and Broadway, Brownwood
24	Comanche	0.25 mi. W of town on U.S. 377/67
24	Bloody fight near Comanche	Indian creek near Comanche, 1861
25	Ft. Blair, CSA	SH 16 at south city limits, Desdemona
26	Snake Saloon	From Thurber, 0.25 mi. N off FM 108 at south county line

About the Authors

Having spent most of her childhood in Florida, Wendi Pierce came to Fort Worth to attend Texas Christian University, where she earned a degree in English, with a minor in philosophy. She then moved to Dallas to earn her Master of Arts in English from Southern Methodist University, thus beginning her career as a professor of writing. After graduate school, she returned to Fort Worth, and in 2003, she began working with Rick Steed on their first book project, *Historic Day Trips from Dallas/Fort Worth*. While her first love is writing, she is also an avid film watcher, and when the weather is just right, she takes a canoe trip on the Brazos with her husband, Reese. Currently, Wendi is a member of the English faculty at Tarrant County College.

Rick Steed graduated from the University of North Texas in 1970 with a bachelor's degree in studio art. Painting north Texas landscapes sparked his interest in its frontier history. Rick has been a member and contributor to the Texas, Oklahoma, Louisiana, Arkansas, Missouri, Colorado, Kansas and New Mexico Historical Societies for many years. Originally, financial responsibilities required in raising a family relegated his artwork in history studies to hobby status. Today, as he approaches retirement age, art and history are Rick's main pursuits, and he considers his investments more like a hobby.

Visit us at
www.historypress.net